Heroine of
the Desert

Heroine of the Desert

DONYA AL-NAHI

with Andrew Crofts

metro

an imprint of John Blake Publishing Ltd
3 Bramber Court, 2 Bramber Road,
London W14 9PB, England

www.johnblakepublishing.co.uk

This edition published in paperback in 2009

ISBN: 978-1-84454-728-9

British Library Cataloguing-in-Publication Data:

A catalogue record for this book is available from the British Library.

Design by www.envydesign.co.uk

Printed in Great Britain by CPI Bookmarque, Croydon, CR0 4TD

1 3 5 7 9 10 8 6 4 2

Papers used by Metro Publishing are natural, recyclable products made from
wood grown in sustainable forests. The manufacturing processes conform to
the environmental regulations of the country of origin.

Some names in this book have been changed for legal reasons.

*This book is dedicated to all the children
who are still out there and want to come back
to their mothers.*

Contents

Prologue

PEOPLE HAVE CALLED me a modern-day saint but once you've read this book you'll see that I am a long way from being that. I'm not proud of everything I've done in my life and I've made enormous mistakes, which I'm happy to confess to. Everyone makes mistakes and there's no shame in that, particularly when you're young. But once you've had children you have to grow up, because from then on you have to put them first, whatever happens. Too often we forget that. We continue with the selfish, thoughtless, careless ways of our own youth, and they are the ones to suffer the consequences of our actions.

I live in a world of mixed cultures, which makes the potential dangers even greater for the children, and I believe that people like me have an extra responsibility to look after the ones we create; to ensure that they don't suffer from any clashes of culture or instability of family roots.

In the end the children are the ones who matter the most and I believe that the thing they need more than anything in order to thrive is the unchallenged right to be with their mothers when they are little and in their most formative years. This is a story about children who have been torn away from their mothers, often in the cruellest ways possible. Their lives have been disrupted in the years when they should be most stable and secure, their faith in their parents undermined as they become pawns in the adults' battles. Helping some of these children and their mothers to be reunited during the years of their childhoods has been the greatest honour for me. It is also proving to be a nail-biting adventure since it often means breaking international laws at the same time as taking on fathers who are willing to fight tooth and nail to keep the mothers away from their children.

I hope that once you've reached the end of the story you will believe, as I do, that it's possible for every one of us to do something positive to help make someone else's childhood happier and safer.

Donya Al-Nahi

CHAPTER ONE

A Mother's Plea

THE WHOLE ADVENTURE started with a polite conversation with a stranger at a bus stop in Queensway on a warm, damp day in 1998. The stop is outside Whitely's shopping centre, a place where I was going to be sitting for many hours and hearing a great many shocking and heartbreaking stories in the coming years.

Queensway is one of those 'melting pot' areas of London; a long road with one end touching the north border of Hyde Park, just a short walk from Kensington Palace and some of the biggest and most expensive houses in London. At the other end lies Westbourne Grove, and all around live people of every race that has ever made London its home, stretching up to the West Indian-dominated areas around Ladbroke Grove and across to Maida Vale and Kilburn. Tens of thousands of families of widely differing incomes and lifestyles live in a hotch-potch of flats and houses, some grand and others cramped and cheaply subdivided in order to accommodate far more people than the original architects ever envisaged.

On one side of this sector lies the West End with all its tourist and entertainment delights, and on the other Notting Hill, which is fast changing from being bohemian and ethnic to becoming as wealthy and fashionable as the West End residential addresses. South of us lie the wide green acres of Hyde Park and north of us sprawl the endless anonymous suburbs of outer London.

Queensway itself has an endearing scruffiness about it and is dominated by shops and restaurants with an Arab flavour. Small grocery stores stand open to the street with their fruit and vegetables piled high on display, the insides of the shops crammed floor to ceiling with unexpected choices of products. Whole families often seem to be serving the customers or talking animatedly to one another when there are no customers. There's a temporary feel about the place, as if many of the residents and businesses are only passing through, making ends meet while they're here, laying plans to return to their homelands or move on to better things. The people may come from a wide range of different countries, but the feel of the place is simply Middle Eastern, from the sounds of the voices to the smells of the cooking, from the Arabic shop signs to the women's headdresses and the music seeping from the shops and restaurants on warm days. It's an area I know well and feel comfortable with. It's the area that has become my home.

Whitely's itself, one of the first and once among the most genteel of department stores in the city, has now become an anonymous shopping mall like thousands of others, full of familiar high street names, covered pavements, escalators, potted palms, water features and floor plans for the confused shoppers. It's a place for locals to shop now, no longer the sort of establishment that would attract customers from other, more fashionable areas of London.

I had all four of my children with me that day, including Alla, my new baby son. Amira and Khalid were both still toddlers and Marlon was a much more grown-up seven years old. Any woman who's been out shopping with four small children knows that you have little time to notice what's going on around you; all your attention is taken up with negotiating doors and roads without losing anyone and trying to anticipate all their needs before they develop into crises or scenes, answering their questions and refereeing their disagreements. But at the bus stop all was peaceful. They were behaving like a model family and I had a few minutes to wait and look around me. I noticed a woman in the queue watching the children with a sad smile on her face and a wistful, far-away look in her eyes. I felt a glow of maternal pride. I smiled at her and said 'hello'. She smiled back shyly and we started talking as we waited.

Like me, and like many other British women in that area of London, she was a converted Muslim. She had a downtrodden look about her that I was familiar with. Her clothes were drab and her face free from make-up. It seemed as if she was unbothered about how she looked, as if she had no pride in her appearance, that it was of no interest to her how others saw her. She had the air of a woman much older than she actually was, someone who had been defeated by the difficulties of life but was still soldiering on because there was no option. She complimented me on the looks and behaviour of my children.

'Thank you,' I replied. 'Do you have children?'

'Yes,' she said and her eyes went down to the ground as if to avoid mine. 'I have a daughter.'

'That's nice,' I said. 'How old is she?'

'She's going to be six soon.'

'Where is she?' I asked. She didn't look like a woman who would have the money to employ a nanny so it seemed strange that she would be out without her child during the school holidays.

'She's in Libya,' she muttered, so quietly that it took me a second to work out what she'd said.

'Is she on holiday?' I asked innocently, not concentrating enough to read the signs she was giving off, a large part of my attention focused on making sure none of the children wandered off before the bus came.

'No,' she replied and I realised with horror that there were tears in her eyes. 'Her father took her from me six months ago.'

'That's awful!' I was shocked, even though I'd heard of such things happening. 'Do you speak to her?'

'I've had only one phone call from her in all that time.'

I felt desperately sorry for her and I could see from her face how much she was hurting, but at that moment my bus came and I was distracted by the needs of the children as I rummaged for money and tickets and struggled to get the pushchair on board and find seats as people in the queue behind us pushed on around us and the irritated driver urged everyone to hurry so that he could get back into the stream of traffic.

That night, at home in Maida Vale, on my way to bed, I went into the children's room and looked down at my sleeping daughter, Amira. She looked so innocent and angelic, her mass of curls spread out on the pillow and her breathing so soft I could barely hear it. I felt a physical ache of love for her in my chest. I remembered with a jolt the woman at the bus stop and it struck me how terrible it would be to have any of my children taken away from me. How unbearable to have to look at their empty beds at night, and in the morning to wake up and sit down to breakfast alone without their noise and chatter. To have to face each long day alone, without any purpose beyond staying alive in the hope that one day you would see them again. I knelt beside the bed for a few minutes stroking her hair in the moonlight, then kissed her lightly on the top of her head being careful not to wake her, checked the others and tip-toed out.

The thoughts wouldn't go away as I got ready for bed. I couldn't imagine how a mother who'd lost a child like that could bear to just stay at home and not do anything about it. If such a thing happened to me, I thought, I'd be on the first plane out to wherever the children were, searching and banging on doors, insisting on seeing them, making so much noise and fuss that no one would be able to keep me out. Or I'd be fighting fire with fire and stealing them back in exactly the same way that their father had, bringing them back to England and going into hiding for as long as was necessary. There was just no way I would have been able to stand the pain of doing nothing and being without them, trying to picture every day how they might have changed, what they might have learned, what they were thinking, what their worries were but not being able to do a thing about it. How would I be able to bear not even knowing the simple details of their daily lives like what they ate for their breakfasts, or what comforters they took to bed to cuddle, or who their school friends were? How unbearable would the agony be on their birthdays or other celebrations, sitting alone, staring at old photographs of how they had looked before they left, without any idea what was happening several thousand miles away in their new lives?

I'd met a great many women like the one at the bus stop in the years since I'd become a Muslim and lived amongst Muslim men. I knew that many of them wouldn't have known how to fight back in that situation, or in any other. If they weren't quiet and submissive to begin with, their men had made sure they became so once they were married. Several men had tried to break my spirit in the past and failed, but I knew that made me an oddity amongst Muslim women from foreign cultures. I felt a terrible surge of pity for the woman at the bus stop and found it hard to get to sleep that night, working out how my own husband, Mahmoud, might be able to steal my children and thinking of a hundred different precautions I should be taking to make sure he couldn't. He slept peacefully beside me, unaware of the complicated scenarios I was imagining around him. He was a good man and I knew I could trust him, but then isn't that what all these women would have said about their men just before they found out, too late, that they couldn't? It doesn't do to think about such things in the middle of the night, not if you want a good night's sleep.

I quite often found myself thinking about that woman in the following weeks, sometimes at the strangest of moments. I might be changing the children's beds, or tidying up some mess they'd left behind, or I might just be watching them as they sat round the television or the tea table and I would be overwhelmed with love for them all. Meeting her had made me very conscious of how lucky I was to have my children with me, and how careful I must be not to lose them. I had no reason at all to think Mahmoud was planning to take them away, and I made doubly sure he knew that if he ever did snatch them I would have been after him like an avenging angel, but it still played on my mind. When I talked to him about it he would listen quietly, his dark eyes serious. When I finished he would shrug his shoulders and smile in the gentle way he has, as if to tell me I was talking nonsense and should know better, and I would feel reassured once more.

About five months after the meeting at the bus stop I bumped into the same woman again in Hyde Park. It was a pleasant day and I was walking with the children through Kensington Gardens, enjoying the sun and the company of the children. I recognised her immediately, even though she was dressed like so many other Muslim women in a long, shapeless brown dress and flat shoes, no make-up and her head swathed in a white scarf. She still gave the appearance of someone who'd given up altogether bothering with herself, as if life had beaten her into submission. It was as if she just wanted to be invisible, walking alone amongst all the happy families, her mind a million miles away.

'Hello,' I called out as she passed. 'Do you remember us?'

She jumped, as if I'd woken her from a dream and then smiled shyly when she recognised us.

'Have you heard from your daughter?' I asked, guessing from the look on her face that nothing had changed since our last meeting.

'No,' she shook her head, her eyes moistening. 'I haven't heard a word. When I try to telephone they hang up the phone.'

'That's terrible,' I said, one eye on the children as they disappeared off in different directions. 'You shouldn't let him get away with it. A child should be with their mother. I really believe that. You should go over to Libya and get her back.'

I could see from the hopeless look in her eyes that she had no idea how to even start arranging such a trip for herself.

'Listen,' I said, grabbing Khalid by the collar as he lurched straight towards a man on a bicycle, 'it's difficult to talk now with the children here. Why don't we meet for coffee tomorrow?'

'Yes,' she nodded enthusiastically. 'I would like that very much.'

'Then we can have a really good chat about it all.'

From the enthusiasm of her response I got the impression that she didn't have anyone else she could talk to about it. How hard it must be to suffer a broken heart in silence and on your own. I thought about how much I'd done with the children in the months since I'd last bumped into her, the outings and family gatherings, the doctors' and dentists' appointments, the children's parties and school plays. I thought of all the funny little things they'd said and done and all the achievements we'd shared with them as they learn new skills. All that time she'd just been waiting in a vacuum, staring at pictures of her daughter and watching other people's children in the park, trying to imagine what her own child would be doing at that moment.

'Shall we meet at Café Rouge in Whitely's tomorrow at eleven?' I suggested and she nodded her agreement.

The next morning I left the children with Mahmoud, as he wasn't due to go to work until the afternoon, and caught a bus to Whitely's. She was waiting for me when I got there. It was the first of many such meetings over the coming weeks.

As we sat amongst the shoppers, drinking coffee, she told me her name was Mary and her daughter was called Leila. She went over the events of the last time she'd seen the child as if they had been yesterday. Every word seemed to bring her pain and she kept having to stop to allow her voice to recover enough to go on.

'I dropped Leila off at her school that morning. It was just the same as every other day. I went home to do some cleaning and to prepare some food for lunch. I think I did a little shopping on the way home. She only attended school in the mornings so I went back to collect her at lunchtime, just as I always did, getting ready to spend the afternoon with her. We used to go down to the park whenever the weather was nice.

She liked to watch the people playing with their toy boats on the water. If it was raining we would stay in and watch her favourite television programmes together or play games. My husband was always out with his friends in the afternoons and so it would just be us two.'

Mary stopped talking and took a sip of coffee to allow time to compose herself. I squeezed her hand and said nothing, waiting for her to find her strength. She wiped her eyes, blew her nose and continued.

'When I got to the school I waited, as I always did, with all the other mothers. The children came out past the teachers and they all ran to greet their mothers. You know how they do when they're excited and wanting to tell everything they've done that morning. Leila was usually one of the first to come out but I didn't worry immediately because I thought she must have been delayed in the toilet or was talking to one of the teachers, or perhaps looking for something she'd mislaid. But then the other mothers started to leave with their children and there was just me left standing by the gate.

'I could see the teacher was looking at me strangely and she came over to me. "Where's Leila?" I asked her. "Your husband took her," she replied. I couldn't understand what she was saying. My husband had never done anything like that before. He believed it was a woman's place to do that sort of work. He never seemed to take much notice of Leila. "My husband?" I said, and I must have sounded stupid. "Yes," she said, "he came in soon after the start of the school day to take Leila to a dentist's appointment. Did you forget?"

'I pretended I had forgotten, and for a moment I thought perhaps I had. But I knew Leila didn't have a dentist's appointment and if she did it would have been me taking her, not him. He wouldn't even have known which dentist she went to. I ran away from those school gates as quickly as possible because I felt so foolish and I didn't want the teacher to ask me any more questions. I was desperately trying to think up explanations as to what might have happened. Maybe my husband had decided to take Leila on a treat and hadn't wanted to admit to the teacher that was why he was taking her out of school. I thought of a dozen possible explanations and forced myself to remain calm.

'I went home and prepared her lunch and waited. I told myself that if they'd been on an outing then she would be hungry when she got back. Every minute seemed like an hour, but they never came back. Eventually it grew dark and I was still just sitting there, waiting.

'They were on a plane for Libya by the time I was at the school gates to meet her. I called some of my husband's friends, because I began to think perhaps they'd been in an accident. I must have been becoming hysterical because one of them told me not to worry, that my husband had just gone back to Libya for a visit to his family.

'I tried to phone my husband's family out there and asked to speak to Leila, but they wouldn't let me talk to her. They said she'd gone to bed because she was tired from the journey. I tried again the next day and they said she'd gone out with her father. I kept ringing and ringing and eventually they just told me to forget about her, that they were going to be looking after her from now on. After that they wouldn't even speak to me, just hanging up whenever I called. That was nearly a year ago and I've had no contact with her in all that time. I kept ringing quite often in the hope that one day Leila would pick up the phone and I'd be able to talk to her for a few minutes before they caught us. I just wanted to hear her voice and let her know that I hadn't forgotten her. Then they moved to a different family house and I didn't know the telephone number any more. So now I have no hope of making contact unless they decide to call me.'

She had to stop talking because she was crying too hard. I put my arm around her shaking shoulders and held her tight, trying to think of something to say that would make her feel better, give her some hope. I couldn't think of anything.

Her story followed a pattern I grew to recognise. There were always telltale signs that the women should have picked up on if they'd only known what to look for. The abductions nearly always happened from schools, with tales of doctors' or dentists' appointments, and there was often another man involved: a brother or a cousin or a friend. There had usually been other signs before that, which the women had failed to pick up on. When the fathers, who had probably shown little or no interest in the child when it was a baby, started to ask where the child's passport was and began to show an unusual interest in his or her welfare, they were usually planning something.

Sometimes the fathers' lives were not going well in England; they might have been unable to find work or have become homesick. They were often depressed or began to criticise England and the English and talk nostalgically about home and about the fine, traditional values of their families. Once the men started to think like that about their homelands they would begin to dream about taking their children back there, away from the temptations of the West, to a simpler and purer culture.

Sometimes, as they were laying their plans, they would become unusually solicitous and kind to their wives, making them cups of tea when before they'd never lifted a finger to help. I came to realise that these were all signs that should sound alarm bells in the wives' minds. But it's always easy to see these things from the outside and with hindsight, not so easy when you're living with someone on a day-to-day basis.

In other cases, once the men began to think about going home, they would start to criticise everything about their wives and the way they were bringing up the child. 'Why are you wearing that short skirt? Why have you got so much lipstick on?' All the things they used to say they liked about the women when they first met them they begin to criticise and despise, comparing it unfavourably to the way their mothers and sisters used to behave in their home country when they were young.

Usually a small child needs to have a few of their personal possessions with them when they travel, and mothers sometimes notice these things have disappeared from the house but still don't put two and two together in time to do anything to stop the abduction. One of the reasons I want to tell my story in this book is to help women in this situation to spot the danger signals in time to avert disaster.

At every meeting we had, Mary talked about her lost daughter all the time and I could tell her heart had been broken. I could see she was a good woman, that she'd been doing all the things she was expected to do in her position, that she'd done nothing to deserve losing her only child. Sometimes the English women who married Muslims would slip back into their old ways, perhaps drinking too much or even taking drugs, wearing clothes that their husbands might consider immodest, or going out with other men. I could tell that Mary had never done any of these things. She'd tried to be a good Muslim wife and still she'd been punished in the most terrible way possible.

She told me of all the different people and authorities she'd been to for help but nobody seemed to be taking any notice of her, or offering any sort of lifeline. It didn't seem right to me. The injustice of it made me boil. Why should it be so hard to just get a child back? It had been easy enough for Leila's father to snatch her in England, why should Mary not be able to do the same in Libya? But I knew she'd never be able to do it on her own.

'I'll go and get her for you.' I heard the words coming out of my mouth at the same time as she did. I hadn't thought about it at all, it just seemed to me that it was the only thing to do in the circumstances. If someone had taken one of my children I wouldn't have been sitting around waiting for the authorities to do something about it, I would have been on a plane the next day. But I could see she was too defeated to be able to do anything by herself and too frightened to be able to think what she would do if she ever reached Libya. With that one sentence, I'd committed myself to a whole new way of life.

Once I'd said the words, it was a promise I couldn't possibly break. I couldn't let her down like everyone else had. Whatever the outcome, I had to do my utmost to get Leila back to England. I felt a little twinge of excitement stirring deep inside me, just like the old days of my youth, with all its trips and adventures. For the previous few years I'd been taken up with the full-time task of being a mother and I was beginning to have itchy feet once more. This would be a chance for a bit of excitement and I knew that Mahmoud would be more than capable of looking after the children if I went away for a few days. Suddenly I couldn't wait to get going.

The operation had to be properly planned. However eager I might be to get started, I couldn't risk messing it up by not covering all angles. We would probably only get one chance since, once they were alerted to the danger, the father and his family would spirit Leila away to some secret address in the country, or guard her so closely we would never have another opportunity to reach her. There were always family members living in distant villages or isolated houses, who would be willing to take a child in for as long as was necessary, or would provide guard services. Any family could make a child disappear for as long as they wanted if they were alerted to the potential danger. We had one major factor on our side, in that the family obviously did not view Mary as a threat, not even bothering to speak to her when she rang. They assumed that she would stay safely tucked away in England, abandoned and alone. They would never think she was capable of actually turning up on their doorstep. As long as they thought that, we had the advantage. Once they knew that Mary had made a friend who was egging her on to fight, things would become much harder.

Time was not on our side, simply because we lacked funds and couldn't afford to stay in Libya for a day longer than we had to. Mary had just enough money for the two of us to fly out there and stay in a hotel for a few days, but no more. If I was going to be successful in bringing Leila back I was going to have to act quickly and decisively within the first few days of arriving.

Another reason Mary had been reluctant to go over to Libya was the language, which her husband had never encouraged her to learn. Although she had picked up a few words, they would never have been enough to perform an operation like this. I, however, was fluent in Arabic, having lived for 18 months in Jordan when I was a teenager and been back and forth to other countries in the area ever since. She'd also been to Libya with her husband in the early days of their relationship when he was proudly introducing his new English wife to his family, and so she knew a bit about the situation we were heading into and was able to describe the house where she was pretty sure they were keeping Leila.

My husband, Mahmoud, thought I was mad to be embarking on such an adventure. He just shook his head in disbelief when I first told him and laughed. I don't think he believed for a second that I was serious. When he saw that I meant business he explained exactly how many ways the whole thing could go horribly wrong.

'They'll probably have someone with the girl all the time,' he reasoned. 'How are you going to take her away?'

'We'll just have to wait until there's a chance,' I argued. 'They can't be with her every moment of the day. We'll wait till she goes to the toilet if we have to and get her from there!'

'But the moment they see she's gone they'll be phoning the police and they'll be watching for you at the airports,' he went on.

'Then we'll have to think of other ways out of the country.'

'They'll be watching them all.'

'Then we'll have to move very fast.'

'Donya,' he said changing his tack. 'Do you realise what they will do if they catch you?'

'They won't catch me,' I replied breezily, not feeling as confident as I hoped I sounded.

'If they catch you,' he continued as if I hadn't spoken, 'they will lock you up and throw away the key.'

'I'd better make sure they don't catch me, then,' I replied.

'What about our children? What happens to them if you get locked up for 10 years?'

'I can't let Mary down,' I said, wanting to shut him up, not wanting to even think of such things. 'I've said I'll do it so I have to give it my best shot.'

I knew that everything he said was entirely sensible but I'd given my word to Mary. I couldn't disappoint her now, having built up her hopes. I also felt that it was the right thing to do. This situation shouldn't be allowed to continue simply because it would be difficult or dangerous to resolve. It wasn't long before Mahmoud realised he wasn't going to be able to change my mind and, with his usual despairing shake of the head, he promised to back me up in any way he could. I could tell he was still worried about the danger I was putting myself into, but he wouldn't try to dissuade me again.

Once all our plans were in place, Mary and I flew to Tripoli, the ancient capital of Libya on the north coast of Africa. It felt like a real step into the unknown as we boarded the plane. I had no idea if we would be returning with the child in a few days' time, or sitting in a jail somewhere in the desert. The danger was increased by the fact that Mary was travelling on her sister's passport, because her sister had her own daughter on the same document, which meant we would be able to use it to travel back out with Leila. We knew it would be impossible to get hold of Leila's own passport, as her father would almost certainly have hidden it in a safe place in the house, or possibly even in the house of a friend or relative. Although the repercussions of being caught travelling on someone else's passport could be dire, it would also be preferable to be coming out of the country under a false name in case the alarm had been raised and the Libyan police were on the lookout for us. By using the other passport we were able to get a multiple visa, so no one would be suspicious of us travelling around the country with Leila once we had her.

Tripoli airport was chaotic and exciting. I loved the smells and the heat the moment we stepped off the plane. This was the part of the world I felt most at home in, like some of the places where I'd spent the most exciting and liberating times of my youth. When I arrived at airports like this I always felt that anything was possible. The buzz made me feel alive. As we passed through the terminal I was looking around all the time, trying to see where the security people were and the cameras. It was impossible to tell if there were any systems in place to check who was passing in or out, or whether officials were watching for children being taken out illegally. Even though we had a flight booked out three days later, I wasn't confident that we would be able to get out this way. I thought Mahmoud was almost certainly right and the airports would be the first places they would swoop down on.

However much planning we'd done, most of what happened from now on was going to be down to luck and instinct. My instincts told me that the airport would be the first place they would inform about Leila's disappearance and, once we were inside the buildings, we would have a hard time getting out again if they spotted us. I was beginning to favour the idea of staying out on the open road and trying to drive across a border, or possibly going out to sea, rather than returning to the crowded, claustrophobic chaos of the airport. In an airport everyone is an alien, which gives the authorities a huge advantage.

Once we were outside in the hot, dry, aromatic air, we hired a taxi driver who agreed to take us to the town where Leila's family lived. It was important that we found a driver who would help us since it was likely we would have to confide what we were up to at some stage. I knew that many Arab men would automatically take the man's side in the argument. It would be a disaster for us if we chose someone who then betrayed us at the last moment. There were plenty of taxi drivers to choose from, all talking to us at once, trying to convince us they were the best ones for the job, even though they had no idea what the job was going to entail. I had to make a quick decision with no more to go on than my instincts for spotting an honest and sympathetic face. I went up to a man who I thought looked as if he could be trusted and the others melted away, going in search of other business as I talked to their colleague.

'We need you to stay with us for a few days,' I explained, 'to drive us around.'

'OK,' he grinned happily, pleased to have a few days of solid work.

'How much will that be?'

After a fair amount of haggling we settled on a fee of about £10 a day. It didn't seem like much, particularly as the car was going to act pretty much as our home from then on, but he seemed more than happy. At night we would stay at a hotel, but from early morning onwards we were back in the taxi, parked outside Leila's father's family home where Mary was almost certain Leila would be being kept. The taxi was not the most comfortable of vehicles, the old leather seats full of tears and covered in sticky stains. It had no air conditioning and smelled strongly of a mixture of fuel, hot bodies, stale food and cigarette smoke. We had to sit with the windows open, which gave no respite from the heat outside.

The house was a simple, breezeblock building, obviously not

the home of a wealthy man. That was a relief to me, but not altogether a surprise from what Mary had told me about her husband. The better connected the father's family was, the more likely the alarm would go up quickly once they discovered Leila had gone, and the more likely the authorities would jump swiftly into action and we would be caught. This did not look like the home of a well-connected family, which would mean they would have little power to bribe or bully the authorities into fast action.

All we could do to start with was watch what was going on. We needed to work out what the family's daily routine was, so that we could decide which would be the best time to strike. We didn't want to be pulling at Leila's arm in one direction if her father or grandmother was pulling the other arm in the opposite direction. It was vital that she was not frightened or panicked any more than she had to be. However much we might have wanted to steam in at the first opportunity, we had to force ourselves to be patient. Mary had to keep her face hidden in case anyone coming out of the house recognised her, and both of us had our heads covered. Hopefully, no one would give a second glance to two covered women in a car; it would just look as if we were waiting for our men to join us. The driver proved to be a lucky find. He soon found out what we were planning and wholeheartedly approved, repeatedly telling us that every child needs its mother. He seemed willing to put up with any amount of tedious waiting in such a good cause. I was relieved that my instincts about him had proved right.

We sat with him for the whole of the first day, simply watching. We arrived outside the house just after the sun had come up, when only a few people were beginning to stir and appear on the street, and the occasional dog or cat would venture out from whatever corner it had been sleeping in, stretching and yawning and shaking off the dust of the night. The first sign of action was a school bus, which crawled past the house at 8 o'clock and pulled up on the corner of the road a few yards further on. It already had some children inside; we could just see their heads bobbing about through the dusty windows. The driver honked his horn to let the family know he was there. A few seconds later Leila came running out of the house in a white dress, her sandals kicking up the dust as she crossed the road, and climbed in. I felt every muscle in Mary's body tense up beside me and her hand went towards the door handle as if drawn by a force too powerful for her to fight.

'Not here,' I told her sharply. 'Not yet.'

I could imagine just how she must be feeling. She was seeing her daughter for the first time in a year. All she wanted to do was scoop her up in her arms and cover her in kisses.

'We need to follow her to school and see what happens at the other end,' I explained and she nodded mutely, the expression in her eyes a mixture of joy and frustration at being so close to her child and yet still not being able to hold her.

'If we grab her now they might hear the commotion from the house, or the bus driver might go in and tell them, and then they'd be after us immediately. We need to do it somewhere else, to give ourselves as much of a lead on them as possible. It would be better to take her from the school.'

I'd noticed there were no telephone lines going into the

house, which would explain why Mary had lost contact with her once she'd moved here. That was good too. That meant someone would have to come physically from the school to inform the family what had happened. There would then be another lapse in time before they got to the police and our details were circulated. We would have several hours in which to put a lot of distance between them and us.

All these thoughts were going through my head as we followed the bus on its 20-minute trip to the school, either overtaking or drawing into a parking space every time it stopped to pick up another child. When it reached the school we drew up about a hundred yards away to watch what happened next. There didn't seem to be any teachers or staff waiting outside for the children, so we had a chance of getting to Leila on the short walk between the bus and the school, and it was possible no one would notice she'd gone until they saw she wasn't in class. I pointed all these things out to Mary, but she was more interested in trying to catch one last glimpse of Leila before she disappeared into the building.

We sat outside the building for the rest of the school day, with the driver bringing us food and drink at regular intervals. I wanted to see if the children were brought out at any stage to play or to walk to another building, but they didn't emerge again until the end of the day, when the bus returned to pick them up. The children streamed out of the school and it was impossible to spot Leila amongst the crowd as they were bundled up the steps of the vehicle. When they were all finally loaded up the driver set off slowly on the return trip, his gears grinding painfully and the exhaust belching black smoke, and the teachers returned inside. Our driver started his engine after a few seconds and pulled in, a couple of cars behind the bus. It took the same route as in the morning and we followed it all the way back to the house, parking and watching as Leila ran back up to the door and let herself in. Mary let out a little sigh, which seemed to be a mixture of pleasure at seeing her child and sadness at watching her disappear from sight once more.

The bus drove off, leaving us in a cloud of dust and exhaust fumes. We stayed there until the sun went down to see if Leila came out to play with friends in the street or walked to someone else's house. We saw adults coming and going, presumably after finishing work, but Leila stayed inside. Eventually, once darkness had fallen and the lights came on inside, we decided it was safe to leave her for a few hours and to go back to the hotel to sleep.

Neither of us slept well that night, despite being exhausted. Our nerves were on edge and we kept going over and over our plans, as if we were attempting to convince ourselves that it was all going to work. We finally fell into fitful dozes, anxious not to oversleep. But there was no chance of that.

Just before dawn we got ourselves up, dressed and slipped down to the street where we found our driver waiting, asleep at the wheel. He woke with a jerk as we got in and greeted us with a broad grin and passed a bag full of food for breakfast over the back of the seat. We ate as we drove to the house, repeating the whole process of the day before. Everything followed exactly the same pattern, even down to the early morning emergence of the sleepy dogs and cats. The same bus driver stopped in the same place at the same time and honked his horn in the same way. Once again we sat in the car all day, outside the school and then back to the house, watching and waiting, just in case we were presented with some perfect and unexpected opportunity, or in case we spotted some snag we hadn't anticipated. Everything went exactly as it had before.

That night, as we lay on our hotel beds talking again, we knew that we had to make a decision. It was time to act. Our return flight was booked for the next day. If we wanted to use the airport as our method of escape we had to time everything exactly or we would either be too early and give them time to inform the airport authorities, or we would be too late and risk missing our flight, which would leave us stranded there for God knows how many hours; a sitting target for the family and the police.

'The best time to take her would be as she goes into school in the morning,' I said. 'That's when there are most people about and when no one will notice a couple of extra women. It's possible the school won't even inform the family she isn't there; they may well assume she's stayed at home because she's ill.'

Mary was like a child herself that night, so excited was she at the thought that she might have Leila back in her arms in just a few hours. There wasn't much chance of a good night's sleep that night either.

Once again on the third day we were outside the house in the taxi at dawn, watching the neighbourhood wake up and embark on its daily routine. My stomach was churning with nerves and I'm sure Mary must have been feeling even worse. Neither of us had been able to face the provisions that our driver had cheerfully handed over. Everything went as it had on the previous two days and we followed the bus to school along the same route. Even our normally talkative driver had fallen silent, aware that he was about to be involved in something dangerous. I'd decided we had to tell him exactly what we planned to do, otherwise we ran the risk of him panicking and driving off halfway through the snatch. He'd nodded his understanding and been unusually quiet and thoughtful from that moment on. I still wasn't certain that he wouldn't lose his nerve at the last moment, but there was nothing more I could do. With any luck he wouldn't want to risk losing his money for the three days by driving off and abandoning us at the last moment.

I felt as if I was about to rob a bank, but I knew that what we were planning was the right thing to do. A mother should never be kept from her child, I kept telling myself. We may be breaking the law but we're doing it for humanitarian reasons. I glanced at Mary as we drove along; she looked wild-eyed and close to screaming with the tension as the bus wound its way through the back streets, picking up other children and then heading out into the countryside and on to the next small town. I hoped she wasn't going to lose her nerve and mess everything up. There were moments when I looked across at her and thought she might be about to faint.

When the bus drew up at the school Leila got off as usual. We stopped directly behind, out of sight of the driver's mirrors.

I squeezed Mary's hand.

'It's time,' I said. 'Let's do it.'

She didn't hesitate. She leaped out of the car ahead of me and ran towards the little girl in the white dress. Her veil was streaming back in the wind, revealing her face, and her arms were outstretched. Leila turned from the friend she'd been talking to and saw her mother running towards her. She dropped her books and ran into her arms. Mary swept Leila off her feet and they seemed to cling on to one another for ages. I glanced back at our driver to check that his nerve was holding and he wasn't about to disappear, leaving us with no escape other than to use our own legs. He also had all our bags in the back of the car, including money, passports and airline tickets. If he drove off we'd be trapped in Libya with nothing. He was watching Mary and Leila too, and his eyes were also darting around to see if anyone else was watching. There was nothing I could do at that stage but trust him; I had to focus my attention on getting Mary and Leila back into the car as quickly and discreetly as possible.

Mary kept hugging her daughter to her beside the road, stroking her hair and her face, kissing her and sniffing her skin. Both of them were crying with joy, lost in their own little world. Behind them I saw a teacher was standing at the gate counting the children in. She didn't seem to have noticed anything but it would only be a matter of time before she looked up and saw what was going on. Without stopping to think I walked over and talked to her, trying to distract her as Mary regained her sense of urgency and bundled Leila towards the cab, which was waiting with the doors open.

'I've just moved to the area,' I told the woman, moving to the other side of her so she would be looking at me and away from Mary. 'And I'm looking for a school that would suit my daughter. May I make an appointment to come and see you?'

'Of course,' she smiled sweetly, continuing to count the children as they passed her, but now only half concentrating on the job.

'It looks like a lovely school,' I said. 'The children seem so happy.'

'Thank you,' she looked up at me and smiled proudly. Several children walked past without her noticing. Hopefully that would mean she wouldn't spot Leila's disappearance for a bit longer.

'I can see you're busy just now,' I said, glancing over her shoulder and seeing that Mary and Leila were safely in the car and waiting for me to join them. 'I'll telephone for an appointment later today, if that's all right.'

'I look forward to hearing from you,' she replied politely, going back to the children as I walked at a sedate pace to the car, forcing myself not to run.

As soon as I reached the open door I jumped in, yelling at the driver to go. The taxi sped away from the kerb. I glanced behind and saw the teacher watching, obviously puzzled by the haste with which I'd departed. With any luck it would be some time before she realised Leila wasn't there and then would think she just hadn't come in and was safely at home. It was possible that no one would notice she'd gone until the bus went past the house that evening and she failed to get off it. It looked likely that we would be able to fly out of the country before the alarm was raised after all.

Leila's initial excitement at seeing her mother had turned to fear in the midst of the shouting and the slamming of doors and screaming of tyres. She was throwing up into a carrier bag as Mary hugged her and sniffed the scent of her hair, as if trying to regain every moment she'd lost in the previous year.

'We've got a few hours to spare before they get their act together,' I said. 'Let's drive straight to the local airport and get on the plane to Tripoli.'

I was banking on the fact that, even if the worst happened and they did spot her absence, the police would not be alerting the airport authorities for at least two hours and probably longer. The driver nodded his agreement and headed the car towards the little local airport. Mary was too busy looking after Leila to care what we did; she was leaving the escape arrangements to me now. All the way there it seemed as if every driver on the roads was doing his best to hold us up. Even though I knew it was unlikely the alarm had been raised yet, every policeman or soldier I saw sent a shiver down my spine. I busied myself getting the money, tickets and passports ready to get straight on a plane. If everything went according to plan now we would be out of the country before they even realised Leila was gone. I couldn't believe it was going to be that easy.

The local airport was a sleepy place and no one seemed to be in any hurry to do anything as we bustled in, the driver carrying our bags and Mary carrying Leila.

'Your flight from Tripoli has been delayed,' the man told us when we went up to the desk to check in and I showed him our tickets.

'Delayed by how long?' I asked, my heart sinking.

He shrugged. 'Four hours, maybe more.'

We moved away from the desk to confer.

'I don't think we can afford to take the risk of hanging around the airport for that long,' I said. 'You saw how many officials there were when we flew in. And if the delay stretched on for another four hours, which it easily might, there would be plenty of time for Leila's father to go to the police and have an alarm call put out.'

'So what are we going to do?' Mary asked, her eyes wide with fear as she hugged Leila to her. The thought of being caught and having her daughter taken away from her again so soon must have been terrifying.

'I think we should use the next few hours to get out of the country by car,' I said. 'The border patrols are much less likely to be on the lookout for missing children. As long as we're on the road we're reasonably safe.'

'Drive all that way?' Mary looked aghast.

'I think it's the safest option.'

'OK.'

We went back with the driver to our cab and told him to set off for the Algerian border, a 17-hour drive away. This was how I would be spending many weeks in the future, driving for hour upon hour, just to put as many borders as possible between the children and the families we'd taken them from. It was sometimes hard on the kids, with the heat of the sun, the dust from the roads and the stops for refreshments in terrible, flyblown little cafés and shops with unspeakable toilets, taking showers in the streets to try to rid ourselves of some of the sweat and dust, and buying bread, honey and watermelons to keep ourselves going, trying to act like tourists.

It was hard on the adults too, but I have to admit I felt fantastically alive at those times, constantly alert for signs of danger at checkpoints, watching everyone we met with suspicion in case they made a phone call after we left, or took a note of our car registration number. Everyone is a potential enemy when you're on the run, however friendly and welcoming they may seem when you pull up in the taxi.

As we drew closer to the Algerian border I became nervous that the officials would spot the difference between Mary and Leila and the pictures in the passport that we were claiming was theirs. Mary looked reasonably like her sister, but Leila had grown up in the year she'd been away and didn't look much like her young cousin any more. I knew from experience that children hardly ever look like their passport pictures, because of the speed with which they change, and I prayed the border officials would think that was all it was.

As we approached the checkpoint I felt sick with fear, and was worried I was actually going to throw up and draw attention to us. I glanced across at Mary and she looked equally drained of colour and close to passing out. We'd given the driver his money for all the days he'd been working for us, and I added a generous tip, as I always like to reward people when I think they've been helpful and kind, and supportive to the cause. He'd given me his address and telephone number and insisted that I call him if I ever needed a taxi in Libya again. I promised I would.

'I will take you through the checkpoint,' he said, 'and then you will have to find an Algerian driver.'

I nodded gratefully as we moved slowly towards the guard post, all of us tight-lipped and silent. Leila hung on to her mother's arm, staring up at everyone and everything with big, frightened eyes. Although she didn't understand what was going on she must have been able to sense that her mother and I were extremely tense. The guard seemed to take forever with the people in the lorry in front, peering at the goods the driver was carrying and then going back to the papers. Eventually he waved him on and we slid forward. The driver passed all our documents out of the window. To me even he looked guilty. The official seemed to take forever to get through the pages, looking through the window at Mary and me, both of us with our faces more or less obscured, and then at Leila, who stared back, pressing herself tightly against her mother. Another car drew up behind us and tooted its horn. The official looked up crossly and then went back to studying our papers, as if determined to make the next man wait even longer as a penalty for his rudeness and impatience. Eventually he handed the documents back through the window and languidly waved us on. We were out of Libya and into Algeria.

Our driver took us over to a group of waiting taxis and went into negotiation on our behalf. We waited in the car, watching as they exchanged cigarettes, drank coffee and talked as if they had all the time in the world. I was horribly aware of the checkpoint guards just a few yards behind us. I was desperate to get moving but I knew we had to take our time in order not to draw attention to ourselves. After what seemed like an age our driver came back with another man. He introduced us to our new driver and started unloading our luggage. The new man seemed just as friendly as the one we were leaving and he had agreed to work for the same price. He took us over to his car, which was in just as bad a state as the first one, and we climbed in. I felt a deep surge of relief as we sped away from the border and away from Libya.

We slept in the car that night by the side of the road and I kept imagining I heard the sound of police helicopters coming to take Leila back and throw us into prison. The car seats were uncomfortable enough when we were on the move; trying to sleep was almost impossible, especially with Leila stretched across our laps and the driver snoring loudly in the front. We were so exhausted by the strain of the previous few days, however, that we eventually managed to nod off. The next day we drove around 800 miles across Algeria to Morocco. I thought it would be safer to put a whole country between us and Libya before we attempted to enter another airport. Now that the authorities had had more than 24 hours to get their act together they might well have alerted the authorities in neighbouring countries.

At the Moroccan border they paid us even less attention than they had at the previous one. There were several coachloads of tourists trying to get over the border, and the officials were obviously more anxious to get everyone through so that they could have some peace than to catch any kidnappers on the run.

In Morocco I bought us some new tickets and we flew back to Heathrow, but even when the plane had left African soil, the fear didn't leave me. The sight of the British officials at Heathrow made my stomach churn as much as the actual snatch had done. We were, after all, travelling on false papers and could get into just as much trouble at Heathrow as Tripoli. It was possible they would even send Mary and Leila back to where they'd come from, refusing to believe they were British citizens without their correct papers.

The queue seemed to take forever. Leila had perked up on the flight, excited by the attention she had received from the in-flight staff, and was asking a lot of questions in a loud voice. Once we were on the plane Mary really relaxed for the first time and bombarded her daughter with questions about what life had been like with her father. It was as if she wanted to know every single thing that had happened in the last year of her daughter's life and Leila, being a typical little girl, was happy to furnish her with every last detail. Having spent several hours talking about herself, Leila seemed to be on a high as the plane landed and taxied to a standstill. I didn't bother to quieten her down. I thought she might well act as a distraction as we went past the stony-faced Heathrow officials. There was a woman on duty at the end of our line and I noticed her glancing at Leila as we approached with our papers. My heart missed a beat. She stared me straight in the eyes for a few seconds then looked down at the passport, methodically thumbing her way through it, looking at the many different stamps and visas. Finally she snapped it shut, handed it back and nodded for me to walk on.

I didn't turn back as she did the same to Mary and Leila. I found myself a seat and waited until they joined me, hoping I looked no different or more nervous than the many other travellers milling around us.

When we were finally through and I saw Mahmoud waiting for me on the other side of the barrier, I felt like crying with relief. But we had to keep up the act for a little longer, just in case we were being watched on a security camera. We made our way out to the car park at the same pace as everyone else, careful not to look in too much of a hurry, and drove back into London in an exhausted and happy silence.

Mary and Leila had to disappear and change their names after that for fear that Leila's father would come back and snatch her again. We agreed not to be in contact and I have no idea where they disappeared to. But I will never forget the looks of happiness on both their faces when they were reunited that day outside the school.

It wasn't long before the memories of how frightened and tired I'd been on the trip faded and I found myself missing the adrenaline. I'd enjoyed the excitement as well as the good feeling of reuniting a mother with her lost child. I wanted more of the same and I wasn't going to have to wait long to get it.

CHAPTER TWO

Becoming a Muslim

I REALLY DIDN'T enjoy my own childhood much. It makes me feel sad to say that because it should be such a wonderful time in everyone's life, but it's no good pretending. My mother and I did not have a good relationship and maybe that's why I feel so strongly that children like Leila, who have mothers that love them, should be allowed every chance to be together. Personally, I would have been quite happy if someone had turned up to snatch me away from my family.

My parents came down to England from Scotland when I was too small to remember anything. They had three girls, including me. I was the one in the middle, sandwiched between Sandra and Tracy. My mother was strict with us; whenever she got upset she took it out on us either verbally or physically, and she seemed to be upset most of the time. I think she was trying to use us to exorcise her own disappointment with life, but nothing she did or said ever seemed to make her feel any better; she just remained angry and resentful.

Dad was an engineer in the aircraft business and was away a lot for his work. That meant Mum had to cope with us on her own most of the time, which she seemed to find increasingly difficult as we grew older and less easy to control. Aircraft weren't just Dad's work, they were his hobby and his first love too. We had a big house near Cambridge with several acres of land and he used to restore old planes in the garden, spending hours tinkering, as if they were no more than giant Airfix models. Once he'd got them right he would take them to pieces again with the utmost care, and trailers would come to take them away to some hangar somewhere, where they could be reassembled under his supervision. I guess they were then put on display in museums. With his hands he was a gifted man; emotionally, however, he found it hard to cope with life. He certainly didn't know what to do with my mother and all her anger.

The two of them were always arguing and fighting. They barely seemed capable of being in the same room as each other without falling out, which made for an unpleasant atmosphere for all of us. As the end of the school day approached, my sisters and I never looked forward to going home, as our friends all seemed to. When I see my own children running up the road from school, shouting with excitement, I feel sad that I never felt like that about going home.

We were tightly disciplined, mainly by Mum, and made

to do everything for ourselves: beds made and rooms tidied before we set off for school, shoes polished, table manners immaculate.

There's nothing wrong with teaching children to be independent and self-disciplined, as long as it's done in a loving way. I suppose I should do more of that for my own children, but somehow I haven't the heart. I like doing things for them. I like to see them carefree and happy. I don't want them to live in an atmosphere of constant nagging and scolding. My sisters and I didn't like to bring other kids home for tea because we could never be sure that Mum wouldn't turn nasty on them for something they'd done, or turn on us over some minor misdemeanour and embarrass us in front of our friends.

Mum didn't have many friends of her own, and didn't seem able to keep them even when she did manage to make them. On the rare occasions that any of our friends did come round they had to go home at 6pm and we would be in bed half an hour later. We would still hear other children outside, playing happily for several more hours, as we lay waiting for sleep to arrive. From the moment we got up to the moment we were put to bed, the house was always enveloped in a sour, petty-minded atmosphere.

Mum always told us all that we should marry into money. I guess that was why she was unhappy, because she hadn't married a wealthy man, although we were perfectly comfortably off on whatever Dad brought home. Mum was always very interested in the Palestinian cause and had contacts from that area. I don't how she first made the connection and I never really understood what happened between her and those people, but it's possible that her fondness for that part of the world did seep into me at an early age.

Mum and Dad stayed together until we'd left home, and then they gave up the struggle to be compatible and got a divorce. I think they would have been a great deal happier if they'd admitted they'd made a mistake earlier on. If they had been happier as a couple, we certainly would have been happier as children. I never believe that couples should stay together just because they have children. I do believe, however, that if couples do part, neither of them should make it difficult for the other to have contact with the children.

Having said that, they didn't quite manage to stay together all through our childhoods. At one stage my mother went off with someone else for a year, when I was about seven, leaving Dad to cope with us on his own. He did his best, poor man, even giving up his job so that he would be at home for us. I remember him making us 'hot ice cream', which was his name for mashed potato, little touches of childhood magic that my mother had never managed to conjure up for us. We had to go into day care for a while because it was more than he could manage, but we always went back to him in the evenings. I have no idea what went on between them during that time, but Mum did eventually come back, with no explanation given as to what she had been up to. We were then put on the social services register because of her continuous slapping. So I'm not unsympathetic to fathers who are left bringing up children on their own, quite the contrary, as long as the mother has gone from their lives by her own choice and has not simply been abandoned by the husband and forcibly parted from her children.

Once Mum had returned to us we moved to Bushey in Hertfordshire. Bushey is deep in the northern suburbs surrounding London, just inside the M25 ring road, but culturally a million miles from the cosmopolitan centre of the city. Nothing had improved in their relationship and the family home remained a deeply miserable and divided place. The moment I was 15, I ran away. I'd had enough. I was sure that, whatever happened to me in the outside world, it would be better than life at home; I'd gleaned that much from visiting friends in their homes and from watching depictions of other families on television. Life didn't have to be this miserable. The final straw came one winter's evening when Mum hit me even harder than usual for something trivial and I was left with a large bruise on my head. I thought Dad would do something about it this time – stick up for me and tell her off – but he didn't, as usual. So I stormed out, without even packing a case, and I didn't go back.

Having no idea where to go, I walked from the house to a nearby church in Bushey High Street, intending to go inside for the night and start my new life at first light. Just to complete the picture, there was a light dusting of snow on the streets and I was bitterly cold, making it all the more a Dickensian scene. But I didn't care about any of the physical discomforts, I felt excited by the thought of being free to do whatever I wanted, to go wherever I chose. When I reached the church I found the front door was locked. I walked all round the building in search of another way in, but everything was dark and secured for the night. I was suddenly very aware of being utterly alone, the only sounds coming from the wind in the trees of the churchyard. I went back to the porch, which was sheltered from the snow and out of the wind. I lay down in a corner and tried to sleep, a thousand different thoughts flitting through my mind.

When dawn broke I was already awake, feeling very stiff and relieved that the night was over. I stood up and shook myself like a dog, trying to get the circulation going in my frozen limbs. I was quite determined that by that evening I would have found myself somewhere warm to sleep. I did not intend to repeat that experience in a hurry. As it grew lighter I walked to Watford and wandered around the empty streets until I found a restaurant that was open and serving breakfast to early workers and people on the way back from night shifts. The windows were steamed up but I could still make out the people tucking into cooked breakfasts, making me realise how hungry I was. I could smell bacon and toast and coffee even before I got to the window and it made my mouth water.

I walked in and asked if they had any vacancies for workers. I must have looked a bit bedraggled after a night sleeping rough, but the manageress took pity on me and gave me a part-time job, and a plate full of breakfast to get me started. As I forked in the eggs and bacon and the warm tea thawed out my insides, I felt that my adult life was well and truly launched.

My next problem was finding somewhere to stay until my first wage packet. I rang a friend and told her I'd left home. She wasn't surprised, having been to my house in the past and met my mum. She said she was happy to put me up until I had enough money saved to pay rent on a bedsit of my own. She warned me I would have to sleep on the sofa, but I didn't care, as long as I was away from my mother I was happy to put up with any amount of discomfort, and it was certainly better than sleeping outside in the freezing cold. A couple of weeks later, with a bit of money in my pocket, I was able to move into a bedsit and I was finally independent. My older sister, Sandra, had an Italian boyfriend who came down and gave me some money to help with the first month's rent.

'Do you think I'm doing the right thing?' I asked him, as we stood looking around at the basic little room.

'Absolutely,' he said. 'You should never go back there. You'll be much happier here.'

Encouraged by my example, both Sandra and Tracy left soon after me. From the moment I left home I was happy and, after a while, I was even able to visit my mother and start to build a new, more adult relationship, although we could never exactly be described as soulmates.

My first boyfriend was a student at Watford University called Karim. I was 16 years old and he swept me off my feet. He was very handsome, a Jordanian, and we really liked each other from the first time we met. There were a lot of Arab boys and young men coming to England at the end of the Seventies and the beginning of the Eighties to study and they all wanted to go out with English girls. Many of them came from cultures where girls were covered up from the age of 12 and didn't emerge again until they were married off to someone suitable. Few of them had ever been on a date with a woman before they arrived in England. When they discovered that English girls were willing to have relationships without getting married, and that they wouldn't even have to take chaperones with them on dates, they must have thought they'd arrived in heaven. Some of them, however, still had marriage in mind the moment they got into relationships, perhaps because they were brought up to believe that you should marry a woman if you were sleeping with her.

In some cases, perhaps, they also wanted to get visas to stay in the country after their studies were finished and knew that an English wife would secure them a place in Britain for as long as they wanted. I dare say some of them were also enjoying a bit of teenage rebellion against their families and were hoping to shock them by bringing home a 'sophisticated' Western girl and flaunting her in front of their older relatives.

We must have seemed just as foreign and exotic to these dark, smouldering young men as they did to us, and none of us really knew enough about one another's cultures to make sensible decisions about building futures together. How could we know anything? We were just kids. But kids of a certain age can often get themselves into very grown-up situations. Some girls would fall pregnant, while others would agree to marry these dashing, charming and seemingly wealthy young men without having any idea of what the consequences might be. It would often be several years before people realised they'd made a mistake, by which time it was too late because there were children involved.

I really liked Karim and when he suggested we should go out to Jordan to meet his family I thought it was a great idea. I had no ties in England and I was eager to experience new things and new places. I wanted to see the places that these boys talked about so fondly and find out how they lived before they came to England. I wanted to understand the culture that produced young men like Karim, certain that it would be very different to anything I'd experienced in England. I felt no great affection for my own roots and I was more than happy to leave my own family behind to go in search of something better.

It did occur to me that Karim and I might be moving towards marriage and the thought did not worry me unduly, but I was in no hurry. I liked the relationship the way it was and I just wanted to enjoy it without worrying about the future or committing myself to anything. Whenever he became too serious about our relationship I'd make him laugh and change the subject as quickly as possible. Maybe I made myself more interesting to him by not immediately agreeing to spend the rest of my life with him. He certainly didn't seem to be cooling off at all as I teased him along.

When we arrived in Jordan it all seemed as wonderfully foreign as I'd hoped, and from the moment we stepped off the plane I was enchanted. I loved the heat and the smells and the lively streets that we drove through on the way from the airport, with families doing everything outdoors in the sun or in the shade of parasols and palm trees. It was so exotic and Karim and his family were so kind and considerate to me. There was someone waiting at the airport to collect us and we travelled on out of the town and into the beautiful countryside where his family had their land.

His family home was completely different to any I'd ever known. Not just because it was a Jordanian style of house, built to keep out the heat and to be the home of an extended family, but because it was full of people who cared about one another, who spoke pleasantly and respectfully to each other. It was a completely different atmosphere to the sterile world of resentment and constant complaining, the anger and the explosions of physical punishment that I'd been used to all through my childhood. No one scolded anyone else, or talked about them behind their backs, or shouted at them. Everyone laughed and hugged and shared their emotions and their possessions. All the generations of the family ate together at mealtimes and talked to one another as equals. They were a proper, warm, loving family. If this was the Muslim life, I decided, I wanted more of it.

The house was big, and sat in the middle of a tiny hamlet amid beautiful green farmland, miles from anywhere. All the surrounding houses were occupied by members of the family; a self-contained community linked by blood and history, where everyone knew and loved everyone else and the only strangers in their midst were honoured guests like myself. I was staying under the roof of one of Karim's uncles, who lived in another house in the hamlet, but I was at the big house most of the time, helping the other women when they would let me, or just listening and talking.

The whole family were lovely to me; such hospitality and such wonderful food and smells from early morning till late into the night. I was bewitched from the moment I arrived. I felt totally wanted and involved in everything going on around me for the first time in my life. Karim spoke openly now about wanting me to marry him and his family were encouraging. They seemed to like the idea of having me as a daughter-in-law. I was flattered by their enthusiasm but I still wasn't willing to be rushed into anything. I was aware of just how young and naïve I still was and how easily I could be swept along on the wave of their enthusiasm. There was a whole world out there that I still knew nothing about and wanted to explore before I settled down. My experience of my parents' marriage had left me deeply nervous of commitment. I didn't want to make the same mistakes they'd made.

While I was out there I started to study the Muslim religion seriously and to change my ideas and my attitudes about almost everything. All the things I read and heard about Islam felt right. All the Muslims I met seemed to have a much healthier and kinder outlook on life than the Christians I'd known in my childhood. I began to picture myself marrying Karim, becoming part of his family and living a completely happy and fulfilled life, and the idea of commitment became less daunting. I felt so at home in Jordan I could imagine spending the rest of my life in that beautiful, friendly land, bringing up my children in the midst of their extended family. A tiny voice in the back of my head, however, was making me wait, warning me that I was still too young to make such a commitment, but the voice was growing weaker with every blissful month that passed.

I'd been out there a year and Karim was increasing the pressure on me to make a decision. I was just on the verge of saying yes, even though I was still only 17, when I heard that his brother was coming home from Britain on a visit, bringing his Welsh wife with him. I looked forward to having some new faces around and to talking to a woman who'd taken the same step as the one I was now considering.

When she arrived I was shocked by the way she looked and behaved. She didn't wear the culture as comfortably as the other women in the family who had been brought up with it. She was all dressed in brown, wearing a baggy men's shirt and no make-up or jewellery. She looked defeated, downtrodden and miserable. I watched the way she was with her husband and it didn't seem to be the sort of relationship I wanted. He appeared to be the centre of attention and her role was to do his bidding. It wasn't that he was a nasty man, because he wasn't, it just seemed to be accepted as the way things should be. Even though I still adored Karim, alarm bells began sounding in my head. Would this happen to me as soon as we were married? Would his attitude towards me change once I was his wife? Would I look as downtrodden as his sister-in-law in a few years' time?

I spent a great many hours going over and over the options

in my mind. On the one hand I did want to belong to such a lovely family and to live in this glorious part of the world, but on the other I was worried about giving up my freedom so soon when I had experienced so little of the world. If coming to Jordan had been such an eye-opening experience for me, I reasoned as I lay awake late into the night pondering my situation, maybe there were other places that I would find even more exciting and fulfilling. I was coming to the realisation that I was still too young to take such a drastic step and that I wasn't ready for marriage. I was quite vain and I liked pretty things. I realised I wasn't willing to give all that up and become a downtrodden wife and mother just yet. In fact, I wasn't sure I ever wanted to marry if it meant becoming my husband's servant.

Having been out in Jordan a year, I decided it was time to find out more about myself and the world before I made up my mind about anything and I caught a flight home to England, giving the impression I was simply going home for a visit. In my heart I knew I wouldn't be going back, but the lessons I'd learned about the Muslim way of life were, by then, deeply imprinted in my consciousness, and they would never leave me. I might not yet have found the man I wanted to spend the rest of my life with, but I'd decided on the religion I wanted to adopt for myself and for my future children. It felt comforting to have something to believe in, having been brought up believing in nothing. I'd also learned a language that would never leave me and would make it possible for me to do the things that I was to do in later years.

I returned to England a much wiser and more balanced young woman than when I'd left.

Although I'd told Karim's family I was just going home for a visit, once I was back in England I confessed to him that I didn't think I could marry him. He was extremely understanding and forgiving, and we got in touch whenever he came to England. Neither of us was quite able to make the final break, but we both knew it couldn't go on like this forever, that we would eventually have to go our separate ways and find new people. I guess he knew that marriage to him wasn't really the life for me, but he went on hoping for a while longer.

It would have been so easy to have gone with the flow and married him, staying in the village and living a life like the one his mother and grandmother and many generations before them had lived. It just didn't feel quite right.

I went back to visit his family recently, when I was in Jordan on a mission. They hadn't changed. They were just as welcoming and loving as I remembered them. Karim is happily married with children now. I don't regret my decision. It was the most wonderful place to spend a formative year of my life, but I could never have stayed there for good. Eventually I would have wanted more from life than tranquillity. I think if I'd been in that house in the middle of nowhere for the last 20 years I'd probably weigh about 20 stone by now and Karim would have become one of the most henpecked husbands in the world.

Even after all those years I was able to find the house without a map. It was like a homecoming, a visit to my roots, the place where I started my life as a Muslim, the place where I changed forever from being the sad little English girl from the unhappy home.

CHAPTER THREE

Becoming the Scarlet Pimpernel

WHEN I GOT BACK to England after helping Mary to rescue Leila, I found the word had spread around the West London Muslim community that I was someone who was willing to help mothers in distress when no one else would listen to them. Even though Mary had moved away, friends and relatives must have passed on the news that Leila was safely back with her mother and that she'd been rescued by an English Muslim woman, who hadn't asked for any money for her services.

Different women started approaching me and asking for help in getting other children back, either for themselves or for friends or relatives. I was horrified by how many snatched children there seemed to be. It felt as if half the mixed partnerships in the world had gone wrong at the same moment.

Every time one of these desperate women told me their story I would see the same pattern emerging, with little variations from time to time. Sometimes the women would be like Mary, living in marriages that they thought were safe and sound, only to wake up one day and find that their husbands had gone, taking the child or children with them. These were the most tragic cases because the women had no idea what they'd done wrong and had been given no opportunity to change their ways in order to avert the disaster. If only their husbands had warned them, many of these women would have been willing to do whatever was asked of them in order to keep their children and their marriages together, but they were never told. Maybe if they had been a little less accepting it wouldn't have happened to them, but people can't change the way they are.

Others knew that their marriages had been going wrong, and might even have been the guilty parties in the breakdown, but had never imagined such an outcome, having been brought up in a country where mothers are nearly always awarded the children if the parents separate. Some of these women might have behaved quite badly, drinking or taking drugs or possibly even having affairs. I might not have approved of their behaviour but, whatever their marital sins might have been, I never felt they deserved to be deprived of their children.

Whenever I started to ask the women questions, I would see the tell-tale signs in their stories which should have warned them that their husbands were dissatisfied with their lives in England, with their marriages and with the dangerous Western influences that they saw all around their children. When men become fathers, particularly fathers of daughters, their previously liberal attitudes can change dramatically. Where they might once have been happy to find young girls dancing the night away in clubs, wearing short skirts and make-up, drinking and smoking, they do not want to think of their daughters behaving in the same way. Most Western fathers have no option but to fight it out with their children on a daily basis, but men from Muslim cultures always have the option of removing their girls from temptation's way and taking them back to a culture where they will be more protected and sheltered. There are probably some Western fathers who wish, from time to time, that they could do the same with their daughters.

In some cases the relationship between the Arab man and the English woman had already broken down by the time an abduction took place, and the woman had moved on to a new partner. The father then found it impossible to see his child being brought up by another man, particularly if that man was not a Muslim and had different views about child rearing. I can quite imagine how desperate these fathers must feel. I know they only want to do the best for their children, giving them the same loving upbringing that they themselves enjoyed, but I still find myself siding with the women every time.

However much I might have sympathised with the men and understood their position, I didn't believe that there were any circumstances in which a woman should not be able to see her children, and in most cases I was convinced that small children were better off with their mothers than their fathers, however well-intentioned and loving the fathers might be.

So it became known in the community that I was a champion for women in tug-of-love cases and that I was willing to go out and do something about it, unlike the many well-meaning charities and organisations which have been set up to help in these cases but are seldom able to produce a result. Any group of people that wants to become accepted by the authorities as a charity or official body has to obey the complex international laws to the letter, which means that, even if a mother who comes to them has right on her side, it will take months, sometimes years, to put into practice. No mother wants to be separated from her children for that long, just because the law moves slowly. People heard that I had no such restrictions placed on me; that I was willing to act first and leave worrying about any laws I might have broken until later. They also heard that I didn't charge for helping bereft mothers, unlike some of the organisations set up by ex-SAS men and other military types, which would charge tens of thousands of pounds for their services, with no guarantee of success. Many of the women who could afford those sorts of sums had lost money to these organisations.

The women who were coming to me were always at the end of their tether. They had usually tried every other avenue, most of them having been to the media to make their pleas as well, and didn't know who else to turn to. I realised that by gaining this reputation as a 'child snatcher' I was putting myself and my family in some danger and needed to take precautions. I didn't want any irate fathers turning up on my doorstep in the middle of the night, and so I made sure that as few people as possible knew my full name or where I lived. I was known as 'Dee' to anyone who approached me, and I operated from a mobile phone, giving the number out to very few people, preferring to get their numbers so that I could ring them and protect my privacy and safety.

Even hiding behind all these precautions, dozens of women were still able to make contact with me. They would find me through mutual acquaintances, or would come up to me in the street or at the school gates as I waited for my children to come out, begging me for help. I would take their numbers and promise to call them. I found it impossible to say no to any of them, and if I said I would ring I made a point of keeping my word. I ended up with £400 phone bills every quarter. I never charged anyone any money. They just had to find enough to pay for any expenses involved in the trip, like air tickets, taxis and hotel bills.

My long-suffering husband, Mahmoud, was enormously supportive, and I wouldn't have been able to do any of it had I not felt confident about leaving the children in his care, sometimes for several weeks at a time. He knew me well enough to realise that, now I'd embarked on this course, nothing was going to stop me. If I didn't help these women no one else was going to. They would remain robbed of their children for the rest of their lives and it was an injustice too great to ignore. How could I possibly turn my back on them?

The second rescue that I agreed to undertake was from Morocco. The child was a similar age to Leila. The victims are most often five or six years old, which is the age at which the Muslim fathers start to panic about their children being brought up in a Western culture. Sometimes I've gone after older children, but I've never been asked to rescue a baby, and I doubt if it would be possible.

Fathers don't want to abduct children while they're still that dependent. That's a stage when they're happy to hand over responsibility to the woman, however unsuitable they may have started to suspect she is as a long-term mother. The logistics are too hard for them anyway. It would be almost impossible for a man to board a plane with a crying baby and not attract attention. He would also have to travel with the paraphernalia of nappies, special foods, carrying equipment and toys. It would all be too difficult, and so they wait until the children are old enough to travel without drawing attention but young enough to follow their fathers trustingly wherever they take them.

When their children are babies, the fathers don't mind what country they're being brought up in, and looking after them without their mothers once they get back to their home countries would be too hard anyway. The grandmothers are always willing to help in any way they can, but not many of them want to take on the responsibility of a small baby. It's also likely that the healthcare services for babies are better in the West.

The mother who had approached me about the Moroccan trip was called Debbie. She'd found out about me from a friend and when she managed to reach me I agreed to meet her. She told me her story over the usual cup of coffee in Whitely's. Her little girl had been taken from school, just like Leila, and spirited away into Morocco. Unlike Mary, however, Debbie didn't have an address for her husband's family home. She didn't even know which town he lived in. Sometimes, if the women hadn't been over to meet their in-laws at any stage, they were unable to understand the Arabic names for towns and villages, and so chose to allow their husbands' backgrounds to remain a closed book, asking no questions and developing no interest in anything outside their own domestic set-up. Sometimes the husbands would choose to weave an air of mystery about their past, and would deliberately withhold information from the women, or even feed them disinformation.

'We need to have some idea where to look before we start,' I told her. 'We need the name of a town or village at least, so then we can go searching for the family name, or we can visit all the schools that take children that age. But we have to have something to go on, because Morocco's a huge country.'

Initially she was disappointed. Perhaps she felt I'd fobbed her off, just like everyone else. But I stayed in touch with her, talking to her regularly on the phone and encouraging her to keep trying to find a clue for us to start with. Then one day the lucky break came. She rang me, almost unable to get her words out because she was in such a state of excitement.

'A friend of mine has just rung me from holiday,' she gasped. 'She was in this seaside resort and she's sure she saw Amina on the beach with a family.'

'Then we have to get there as quickly as possible,' I said. 'For all we know they may be on the last day of their holiday. If they go home we might lose them for ever.'

Speed is never a problem. If necessary I can plan a trip and get to the destination within a day, just as long as there are plenty of flights.

Twenty-four hours later Debbie and I were ensconced in a beachside hotel in the resort where Amina had been spotted. Debbie was almost beside herself with excitement, firstly at the speed with which everything was happening and secondly at the thought of seeing her daughter again after so many months of separation. Both of us were tired from the trip but we couldn't afford to waste any daylight hours sleeping. We were going to have to be searching for every hour that there were children out and about. It wasn't a large beach area and we could see most of it from the balcony outside our room.

As I stood beside Debbie, leaning on the railings and looking down at the dense crowd below, I felt a terrible sinking feeling. How would we ever pick Amina out at this distance from so many similarly coloured children? There were dozens of dark-haired little kids sitting on the sand or running happily in and out of the surf. It was like staring at one of those 'Where's Wally?' pictures, where you have to pick out one tiny person from an immense crowd scene. Debbie was scanning the scene with a look of fierce intensity, almost as if she was willing her daughter to appear before her eyes.

'Maybe we should get down there and walk about a bit,' I suggested. 'It's really too far to be able to pick her out from up here.'

'No.' she shook her head adamantly. 'I'll be able to spot her if she's there.'

I admired her confidence but I wasn't so sure. I decided that, with her in this mood, there was no point arguing and waited patiently on the balcony beside her, enjoying the sunshine and the busy, happy holiday scene going on below us. As the afternoon wore on and the heat of the sun relented a little, more families made their way out of their cool villas and hotels, their children refreshed by afternoon naps. Debbie continued to scan back and forth like a radar antenna.

'If we don't get down there soon the light's going to have gone and we'll have to wait till the morning,' I warned.

'There,' she shouted, pointing and almost leaping over the balustrade in her excitement. 'That's Amina, there!'

'Where?' I peered down in the direction she was pointing, unable to make out any individual.

'With the three women and those other children. They're sitting on the chairs and she's running down to the water in a red rubber ring. Do you see?'

Now I could see the child she meant, but it was too far away for me to be able to make out her features.

'Are you sure it's her?' I asked.

'Yes. Come on, quickly, we have to get down there and get her.' She was already running back into the room pulling a scarf around her head.

'Wait,' I shouted. 'If we go charging down there now they'll know we're here and we have no escape route ready. If you frighten them they'll disappear off and we'll never see them again. Take it slowly. You stay in the background and I'll get talking to the women to find out how long they're going to be here and how long we have to work in.'

She paused for a second and glowered at me, obviously not wanting to suffer any more delays in being reunited with her lost child. I said nothing, just stared back and after a few seconds she relaxed.

'OK,' she said. 'You're right. I'll hang around in the background and keep my face covered.'

We made our way downstairs and out of the hotel on to the seafront road, sauntering across to the beach as casually as both of us could manage. Debbie sat down a little way behind the party with Amina in it, and I moved closer to them. I spent a few minutes watching Amina playing in the sea with some older children who I guessed were her cousins. The other children were being very kind to her, as if she was a family favourite, and she was bossing them around mercilessly, as little girls do when they know they are the centre of attention. One of the women was older than the other two and seemed to be in charge. I caught the older woman's eye and we both laughed at her antics.

'She's a beautiful little girl,' I said. 'Is she yours?'

'My granddaughter,' she said, beaming with pride. 'She loves the sea.'

'She looks very at home in it,' I said. 'Do you live in this town?'

'No, we're just here on holiday. We're going home the day after tomorrow.'

'You'll be sad to leave the beach,' I said to Amina, who had come running up to show her grandmother some treasure she'd found in the surf.

'Grandma says we can spend all day tomorrow down here,' she told me, puffing her little chest out as if challenging me, or her grandmother, to deny this fact.

'Yes, Amina.' The old woman laughed and squeezed the little girl's sandy hand lovingly. 'We will spend all day on the beach.'

I made small talk for a little longer with the other women and then bade them all goodbye. I wandered back up to the road as casually as I could. Debbie followed a few moments later, catching me up just as I reached the hotel. I could see she'd been crying, but she wasn't sad, she was almost hysterical with joy at having found the daughter she was afraid she'd lost forever.

'What did you find out?' she asked as we went into the hotel lobby.

'They're going to be on the beach tomorrow,' I told her, 'but they're going home the following day, so we need to act quickly.'

'What will we do?'

'We need to make sure we have a car ready,' I explained. 'And book tickets back on the afternoon flight.'

The next morning I wandered out of the hotel to talk to a bunch of taxi drivers sitting in some nearby shade. I found one that I liked and asked him to keep himself free for the whole of the next day. He was happy to agree and gave me his telephone number, telling me to call when I was ready for him.

'You have to be able to get here within a few minutes of me calling,' I warned him.

'Sure,' he smiled reassuringly. 'No problem.'

Debbie and I then watched the beach from our balcony and went down as soon as we saw Amina and her paternal family arrive. Debbie covered herself up again and sat in the same

64

place as the day before. I'd also covered myself so they wouldn't recognise me and sat between her and the family group so that I could hear what they were saying, since she didn't speak any Arabic. They didn't seem to take any notice of me and made no attempts at conversation.

The morning passed happily with the children playing and the women talking amongst themselves. After a while one of them said she was hungry and another agreed. They began to discuss what they wanted to eat and I realised they were planning to buy sandwiches from a nearby stall.

'They're about to go and get some sandwiches,' I whispered to Debbie. 'This may be our best chance, while they're distracted.'

I had the familiar churning of fear and excitement in my stomach as we waited for the women to make up their minds about what they were going to buy. Amina was still down by the shore, collecting sand in a bucket and trying to build sandcastles, which the water was destroying as quickly as she made them. The older children were swimming in the water a little further out and didn't seem to be taking any notice of her or anyone else on the beach. Finally the women made up their minds and stood up, making a big show of dusting the sand from their robes. They glanced down to the sea to check that everything was all right and then turned towards the snack bar, which was about 20 metres away at the back of the beach.

'Go quickly,' I hissed to Debbie. 'Take her to the hotel room and I'll join you there once I've seen what they do next. When you get to the room ring the driver and tell him we're ready to go.'

Debbie didn't need telling twice. She ran down to Amina and I watched as she pulled back her scarf to reveal her face. The little girl dropped her bucket and threw her arms up with a shriek of pleasure as Debbie lifted her up and hugged her close. I glanced back up the beach to see if the women had seen or heard anything but they were all facing the man behind the counter, gesticulating and pointing at the food, giving him instructions as to exactly what they wanted. The other children in the sea were too busy splashing around to notice anything as Debbie started walking away with Amina clinging to her like an excited little monkey. Other children moved into the gap where she had been playing and it was as if she had never been there.

I shifted back into a more crowded spot so I could see what happened next without drawing too much attention to myself. Debbie was at least a hundred yards along the road towards the hotel by the time the women started walking back with the food, chatting amongst themselves about their purchases. From the back it was impossible to tell that she was carrying a child in the loose folds of her long dress. The women sat back down and began eating and passing the food to one another. One of them waved to the children in the sea to tell them to come in for lunch. Then the grandmother asked, in a loud voice, where Amina was. The other women glanced up, not too concerned at first, more interested in their meal. They all looked up and down the beach for a few moments and then climbed to their feet to get a better view, shielding their eyes from the sun with their hands and scanning further afield.

Their voices grew louder as they became more agitated and they all ran down to the water's edge, shouting for the other children to come in quickly and calling out Amina's name. I glanced anxiously back at the road but there was no sign of Debbie. She'd made it safely into the hotel.

Now there was full-scale panic on the beach. The women were scouring the sea, imagining Amina must have drowned. The other children had swum in and were being berated for not taking care of their young cousin. Other people on the beach were hearing the commotion and being dragged into the discussions on what to do for the best. I listened intently to what was being said but no one seemed to have noticed the little girl being picked up by Debbie. The grandmother was starting to cry and I felt very bad for her. She obviously loved Amina and, hopefully for us, it would be some time before she would discover that the girl was safe and with her mother in England. I could just imagine how terrible she would be feeling, believing the child had drowned while in her care. Even when she found out the truth she would still feel responsible for allowing Debbie to snatch Amina away from under her nose. I would have loved to reassure her that everything was all right, but I knew I couldn't, not without endangering the whole mission.

They weren't taking any notice of me, an anonymous, covered woman on the beach with no child attached to her, so I slipped away and joined Debbie and Amina in the hotel room.

'The driver says he's half an hour away,' Debbie told me as I walked in, obviously in a terrible state of nerves, mixed with elation at having Amina back. 'We're going to miss the flight at this rate.'

'Why is he half an hour away?' I wanted to know. 'I told him to be ready all day.'

'I think he thinks that is being ready.'

There was nothing we could do. It was too late to find another driver who we could rely on to be discreet. I went down to the lobby to wait with our luggage so that we could run straight out when he arrived, leaving Debbie and Amina in the room in case anyone from the beach came in to ask the hotel if they'd seen a lost child. I could see from the door that there was still a lot of activity on the beach. The police had been called and were beginning to join in the general melee of shouting and gesticulating. It looked like chaos. Sooner or later they would be searching along the road and going into the buildings. We needed to get away quickly.

Half an hour passed and the car still hadn't arrived. I phoned the number for the driver and some woman told me he was on his way and that I shouldn't worry. When I asked how long he would be she said 'soon'.

There was now only a couple of hours before our flight left, and there wouldn't be another one until the following morning, unless we flew to another destination, but we were carrying hardly any money and would have looked out of place flying into Paris or Amsterdam with a child and British passports. The chances were the police would have circulated Amina's picture to the airports by the following morning, unless they remained convinced she'd drowned, which they probably wouldn't once they'd been told she had an English mother. It wouldn't take the police long to put two and two together. All these thoughts were spinning around in my head and I found it impossible to think straight. I paced back and forth by the doors.

There was still no sign of the car and I was beginning to think I would have to go out and hail one in the street. But what if the driver I hailed had been on the beach and knew there was a small child missing? I decided that wasn't an option.

An hour after we got back to the room the driver arrived, looking as if he didn't have a care in the world. He just shrugged when I gave him a piece of my mind and gestured vaguely towards the traffic outside, which seemed to me to be moving perfectly normally.

I told him to load the luggage and wait in the car right outside the front door of the hotel. I rang up to the room. Because I'd already settled the bill and our cases were gone, when Debbie and Amina got downstairs we were able to go straight out to the car without attracting any attention from the staff.

'Please get us to the airport as quickly as you can,' I said to the driver as Amina curled up with her head in her mother's lap, so she wouldn't be visible to any passers-by. There were still some police cars parked along the edge of the beach, although the crowd was thinning out now. The driver gave us a broad and charming smile, as if he was anxious to please in any way he could and we set off at a steady speed.

'How long to the airport?' I asked.

'An hour, maybe an hour and a half, depending on the traffic.' He shrugged again.

'We need to be there faster than that,' I said. 'We have a plane to catch.'

'Leave it to me,' he replied and pushed the accelerator to the floor.

We hurtled round corners and through towns at speeds that must have been double the limit, and I dreaded hearing the sound of a police siren coming up behind us, but I dreaded missing the flight even more so I kept quiet. When we finally came to a halt in front of the airport we had 45 minutes to spare until the plane took off. We ran to the check-in counter just as they were about to close it. They were in such a hurry to process us through that they didn't look too closely at Debbie's and Amina's passports, which was just as well as they weren't their own, and we were ushered through the airport and on to the plane as they were closing the doors.

I was shaking with nervous exhaustion as we took off and I saw the sea appearing below us. Amina was chatting happily to the stewardess and Debbie was watching her with a proud, relieved maternal smile on her face. It was an expression I hadn't seen before. It was as if she'd lost ten years in as many minutes.

The adrenaline was pumping through my veins as I sat back in my seat and took some deep breaths. I'd managed to make a second successful rescue. I felt invincible. I felt like the Scarlet Pimpernel, the fictional eighteenth-century character who used to rescue French aristocrats from the guillotine during the Revolution and whisk them away to safety in England.

CHAPTER FOUR

My Own First Escape

ONCE I'D LEFT HOME at 15 and was in charge of my own destiny, my relationship with my mother improved considerably. Neither of us quite approved of the other, or was ever going to forgive or forget the things that had been said and done on both sides over the years, but we were able to spend time together and occasionally even go on holiday like a couple of girlfriends – well, nearly.

It was when we were on a beach holiday in Tunisia, not long after my return from spending a year with Karim's family in Jordan, that I met Ahmed. Everyone warns you against holiday romances, but that doesn't make them any less attractive. When you're in an exotic foreign country, relaxing and enjoying yourself, life seems different and your sense of judgement becomes distorted. You make decisions you would never make in the grey light of home, and form friendships with people who you might never have bothered with if you were busy with the distractions of your own life.

Ahmed's father was from Qatar and his mother was from a big farming family in Tunis. He was a skinny, puny little guy, but somehow he caught my attention. I was 19 years old and still had feelings for Karim, who I'd seen several times in London since returning there and was still getting over. Whether or not it was a rebound situation, I was certainly confused about my own feelings; did I want to be footloose and fancy free, or did I want to commit to a relationship and start a family? Sometimes I was sure it was one, at other times equally certain it was the other. No doubt such contradictory feelings are typical in a 19-year-old girl, but that doesn't make them any less difficult to cope with at the time, particularly if you have a mother whose opinion you don't exactly respect and whose advice you're inclined not to seek.

Whatever my state of mind at the time, when Ahmed asked me to marry him I convinced myself I'd fallen in love and that marriage was what I wanted. Maybe it was the heady scent of jasmine on the Tunisian night air or the romanticism of the souks and the camel rides along the beaches; maybe it was little more than a holiday romance. Whatever it was, I went and said yes, and almost convinced myself that I meant it.

My mother was happy to encourage me, seeing it as a way to get rid of Karim once and for all, since she had never thought he was wealthy enough to be good husband material, and replace him with someone who had some money. Ahmed lived in a big house in Tunis and drove a BMW. He had all the qualities that my mother looked for in a prospective son-in-law. Ahmed's family were also encouraging the match, so there was no one for me to air my doubts to when they started niggling at the back of my mind in quieter moments.

Both Mum and I had always liked the idea of a formal wedding. Ahmed's family were happy to pay up for a big pre-wedding party in the Tunisian style and Mum ordered a full-scale white wedding dress from Berketex in London, which she and my sister, Sandra, brought out to Tunis for me. The bandwagon was rolling and it looked as if this time I was going to go through with it.

I felt increasingly nervous but assumed it was the way every young bride feels as her wedding day approaches. 'You've got to make a commitment sooner or later,' I told myself, when I should have been telling myself, 'You're only 19, for heaven's sake, you don't have to make any commitments to anyone if you don't want to.' It's all too easy to let life sweep you along instead of taking control of the situation. I guess that's what happens to so many of the young English girls who marry Muslims from the Middle East or Northern Africa. Probably they feel qualms and doubts about what they are doing, just as I did, but it is simply too difficult to stop the impetus once it has got going. Maybe some of them do receive warnings from friends and relatives about the dangers of what they are doing, but continue as an act of rebellion, determined to prove that those who are advising them are ignorant or racist or narrow-minded. That determination probably overrules any voices of doubt or disquiet that might be sounding off in the backs of their own minds. They've made a stand in the name of love and so they have to stick to it, come what may.

On the day of the wedding, as the guests assembled for the lavish pre-ceremony party, my doubts were reaching a crescendo inside my head and making me feel sick with tension. On the outside I might have looked like the picture-book bride, but on the inside I was a mess. I was having difficulty focusing on what was going on around me. There seemed to be hundreds of people swirling past as I sat amongst them in my wonderful white wedding dress and jewellery, accepting a kiss on the cheek from this uncle and a tearful hug from that aunt. They were all so sweet and kind and welcoming and they were all having such a good time I didn't know what to say to any of them. I felt quite giddy as the party came and went around me. Just as the room seemed as if it wouldn't take a single other person I turned and caught a glimpse of the bridegroom entering in all his wedding finery. I did a double take. I didn't recognise him, and for a moment I couldn't work out why. Then I realised; he'd had his hair straightened for the ceremony. If he'd looked puny before, he now looked positively strange. All the doubts that had been nagging at the back of my mind came galloping to the front. The sight of this poor eager little geek jolted me to my senses and I realised I was about to make a serious mistake.

I had to make an instant decision or I was going to end up married to a man who looked so ridiculous on our wedding day

I would never be able to think about it without laughing – or possibly crying. I knew it was impossible to continue but I didn't know how to stop it. Should I stand up and make an announcement to the assembled crowd? They'd probably lynch me there and then. Should I go up to Ahmed and come clean? But then he was bound to beg me to change my mind and I would be in an impossible position. In the end I hadn't the heart to spoil their party or the nerve to face up to Ahmed. I stood up and moved through the crowd like a sleepwalker, allowing them to squeeze my arms affectionately, hug me, admire the dress, tell me how beautiful I was and how lucky Ahmed was, and wish me the best of fortune. Some relatives of Ahmed's I'd never met before were introduced to me halfway across the room and I enquired politely how their trip to Tunis had been. I don't recall their answer.

All the time I kept walking, almost in a dream, towards the door that my groom-to-be had come through a few minutes before. It was the longest walk of my life and I dreaded bumping into Ahmed on the way and having to look into his face and see how happy he was to be getting married. I reached the door, opened it and went outside. No one said anything or tried to stop me. Perhaps those who saw me go thought I was just popping out for a breath of fresh air. Some of the women probably exchanged knowing looks, remembering how nervous they were on their own wedding days. I carefully closed the door behind me and the noise of the party disappeared abruptly. My first thought was to get away from the scene before anyone else came out and asked me what was wrong. I wasn't in the mood for explaining anything to anyone. I hailed a passing taxi and climbed in, squashing my meringue of a dress around me in the grubby back seat. There were brightly coloured lucky charms and religious artefacts dangling round all the windows, giving the car a celebratory air.

I told the driver the name of a modest hotel I knew in another town, where I was pretty sure they would give me a room even though I was arriving in a wedding dress with no money or luggage. I had some jewellery on me, which I gave to the taxi driver as an advance on his fare. I was desperate to get away from the area before Ahmed and his family realised what had happened and came looking for me. They would all assume I'd been taken ill and fuss over me and give me no space to explain in their anxiety to keep the show going.

I glanced over my shoulder as the taxi pulled away but the door to the party was still tightly closed. It would probably be some time before they realised I was gone. I felt so sorry for Ahmed. He'd been so kind to me and now I was going to make him terribly unhappy and embarrass him in front of all his friends and relatives.

When we arrived at the hotel I checked in, still wearing my wedding dress, but no one said anything. I was shown to a room and once I was safely inside I made contact with some friends in the country, just to hear some friendly voices, and after a few hours I rang my mother at her hotel. I was dreading telling her what I'd done, but she was much more understanding than I'd been expecting.

'I don't have my passport,' I wailed. 'It's back at Ahmed's house, along with all my other things.'

'Don't worry,' she said. 'We can sort it out.'

I was touched by her protectiveness of me, but couldn't see how she could possibly straighten out the mess I'd got myself into.

'I'm not going back there,' I said categorically. 'I just want to get back to London.'

'It's all right,' she tried to soothe me. 'I have some Palestinian friends in Tunis. They'll be able to get hold of another passport for you.'

I'd never really understood why she had so many Palestinian friends and I'd always been rather dismissive whenever she mentioned them, but now I was extremely thankful for anyone who could offer me a way out. I went to bed and slept fitfully. I was partly relieved to have got out of a marriage that I'd been becoming increasingly nervous about, and partly troubled with guilt at what I'd done to Ahmed simply by rushing into things without thinking them through.

The next day my mother joined me at the hotel and a succession of shady-looking men came and went, leaving us with some money and a passport that would get me back to England. We slipped quietly out of the country a few days later.

I never heard from poor Ahmed or his family again. I hope he managed to meet a nice girl and is now happily married with hundreds of children. I'm sure I wouldn't have been a good wife for him. Even if I'd gone through with the ceremony

I would have left him by now. I would never have been willing to stick at the marriage simply because I'd been through the ceremony, and he would have ended up being much more unhappy. I hope he realises that he had as narrow an escape as I did that day.

Once I was safely back in England I still felt an enormous attraction to the Arab lifestyle. The warmth of the sun and the warmth of the people had soaked into my memory and made London seem dull and grey. Over the next couple of years I took every opportunity to go out to the Middle East or North Africa for holidays, and most of the new friends I made were from that part of the world. On a trip to Kuwait I met a man called Mohammed, who was to become one of my greatest friends and confidantes in the coming years. Nothing ever happened between us but he always said I should have married him, that it was meant to be. Sometimes I think perhaps he was right, but I believe it would have spoiled our friendship if it had gone any further.

Male friends like Mohammed taught me how the Arab man thinks and what he feels about himself, about his family and about women. There is a misconception in the West that Muslim men don't respect their women, fed by horror stories like the way the Taliban treated women in Afghanistan. But in Islamic law the woman is revered, even more than the man because of her childbearing abilities. Life is hard for many of them, but then life can be hard for the men as well. There are those who are downtrodden and treated as second-class citizens, but I could find you a good few women who fit that description in the West as well. The men almost worship their mothers and grandmothers and the older women have enormous status within their families, something you seldom see in the West where the old are seen more as a nuisance and a liability.

Arab men also respect their sisters, and most will respect their wives and daughters as well if they behave in a way that they can understand and feel comfortable with. But when they come up against Western women who, to their way of thinking, don't seem to respect themselves, they're left confused and sometimes angry. Once the initial sexual attraction has dimmed they want to show these women the error of their ways, persuade them to behave with more dignity, like the mothers and sisters they so revere. Not surprisingly, many of the more spirited Western women object to being told what to do and how to behave. Their culture has not prepared them to be lectured on how to dress, what make-up to wear, where they can go and who they can befriend. In time the culture gap becomes a chasm into which any children who might be involved fall.

CHAPTER FIVE

A Girl Behaving Badly

WHEN WE'RE YOUNG we sometimes get into relationships we shouldn't, and we sometimes do things we shouldn't – at least I know I did. It can at times lead to unfortunate consequences, particularly when people marry or have children too soon, but it's inevitable. It's part of the growing-up process – part of learning who you are and where your limits lie.

Soon after my holiday in Kuwait my younger sister, Tracy, was driving me back down into central London after a visit. My mother was in the car and I fancied some chocolate so I asked my sister to turn into a service station. As usual there was a bit of bickering going on in the car, although I can't remember what it was about, so I was glad to get out into the fresh air, albeit amongst the petrol and exhaust fumes.

I made my way into the brightly lit shop, chose my sweets and went to queue at the till. As I was paying I dropped a penny on the floor. I went on with the process of paying and ignored the fallen coin.

'Excuse me,' a man's voice said behind me, 'you've dropped some money.'

He smiled and bent down to pick it up. As he straightened up and passed me the penny I took in his face. He looked nice. Nothing special, but nice, with a mass of thick, dark curls framing a friendly face. I looked down at his clothes. He had on trousers that were too long for him, trainers, a V-necked jumper and a shirt. I guessed he was an Arab and that immediately made me more interested than I might otherwise have been. My sister had come in after me, probably to get away from Mum's voice for a few moments, and was standing beside me. She was oblivious to what was happening with the man, rattling on about how she didn't know if she would be able to drive me all the way home and that she might have to drop me at a railway station because she had to get somewhere else. She was getting on my nerves.

'That's fine,' I said, only half-listening to whatever she was saying. I turned back to the man. 'Are you going down to London?' I asked.

'I am,' he replied very politely.

'Can you give me a lift, please?'

'Certainly.' He smiled and didn't bother to ask where in London I wanted to go.

My sister and I went back out to the forecourt and I

fetched my stuff from her car while my Good Samaritan paid for his petrol. Clutching my overnight bag I looked around for his car and saw an old banger standing by the next pump waiting for its owner to return, which I guessed must be his. I waved goodbye to my mother and sister and made my way towards it. As I got closer to the car he came out of the garage and turned in a different direction, beckoning me to follow. I looked across to where he was heading and saw the long sleek shape of a red Lamborghini, all the lights of the service station reflected in its gleaming paintwork. I couldn't stop myself from laughing; it was just such a surprise and such a cliché.

I lowered myself into the white leather passenger seat as he held the door open for me, like a real gentleman, and he then walked round and climbed in beside me. I watched my mother and sister driving off, my mother's chin practically in her lap. All my life she'd been telling me and my sisters that we should marry rich men, so I guess there were cash registers going off inside her head like fireworks as she watched us overtake them on the motorway in a turbo-charged flash of shiny red steel.

As we came into north London, much sooner than I expected, we passed a Persian carpet shop which was near to a restaurant I'd recently been waitressing in. I'd passed the window dozens of times on my way to and from work and each time I'd been drawn to the beautiful patterns of the rugs and carpets on display. I pointed the window out to my Good Samaritan as the Lamborghini growled past, its engine seemingly irritated to have been made to slow down by the weight of traffic, and he drew up into a parking space.

'Show me this shop,' he said, and we climbed out.

Despite the late hour it was still open and the owner brought out dozens of carpets for us to look at. In the end my new friend bought me a beautiful little mat embroidered with a delicate pattern of tiny birds. It was a charming gesture and I warmed to him even more.

He took me to see his apartment in Upper Grosvenor Street, a road deep in the heart of Mayfair, running between Park Lane with all its grand hotels and Grosvenor Square, which houses the American embassy and some of the finest terraced mansions in London. We hit it off immediately and started going out quite regularly. At the time I was without a home and had been living with my mother in Bushey, which was proving to be almost as much of a disaster as living with her as a child had been, since we could hardly bear to be civil to one another for more than a minute at a time. Quite soon after we started going out I told my new boyfriend about the situation at home and how uncomfortable it was.

'So, why don't you move out if it's so terrible?' he asked, genuinely perplexed.

'I can't,' I laughed. 'I don't have any money.'

The idea of not having enough money to do whatever you want whenever you want was obviously alien to him. He shrugged as if the answer was so obvious he couldn't think why neither of us had thought of it before.

'I will buy you somewhere to live,' he said and, true to his word, he bought me a house right behind my mother's, which cost £72,000. It was an area that I knew and felt reasonably comfortable in, and it put a bit of space between my mother and me, although I could still overlook her garden from my upstairs back windows. She was gutted, which made it all the more satisfying.

I lived very happily in that house, which had a lovely garden, and my relationship with the wealthy young Saudi continued to blossom. I became somewhat pampered, and enjoyed the feeling. He bought me a Persian cat to keep me company on the nights when we didn't see each other, and used to drive out to pick me up for our dates in London. I decorated the house from top to bottom with luxury furnishings at his expense and he didn't bat an eyelid. He took me on some wonderful holidays to the sorts of places where the rich go to play, and treated me for all the world as if I was the main person in his life. I had everything I needed for a comfortable life but I wanted more. I started to become greedy.

'I'm flying home to Saudi Arabia,' he said one day. 'I'd like you to come out with me and meet my family.'

I was very pleased. I always enjoyed meeting Arab families, even if the encounters had ended unhappily a couple of times. I had wonderful memories of hospitality and kindness, which I treasured, and I looked forward to collecting new ones. I was also intrigued to learn more about a man who seemed to have unlimited amounts of money but didn't appear to have to work for it.

He'd mentioned that his family wanted him to marry a

cousin of his. 15 years older than him, she was divorced and already had two children. I thought this invitation to go out to Saudi suggested he might be willing to confront them and tell them he wanted to marry me. I don't think I was any more sure that I wanted to marry him than I had been with Ahmed or Karim, but I certainly liked the idea of being asked and of usurping this other, powerful, unseen enemy. I liked him, so maybe I did want the relationship to go further.

We headed for Jaeger and bought all the clothes I needed for the trip, plus the cases to pack them in. I was beginning to get in the mood for this new adventure. We were all set to go when a call came through for him from Saudi.

'I'm so sorry,' he said when he came off the phone. 'My mother has suffered a heart attack. I'm going to have to return on my own. It would not be an appropriate time to introduce you to my family. I hope you understand.'

Of course I understood, but that didn't mean I wasn't severely put out by his mother's unfortunate sense of timing. I could see that he was right about going on his own, even though I was disappointed and would miss him while he was away. It would hardly be diplomatic to present his mother with the woman he wanted to marry when she was in such a delicate state and desperately wanted him to marry another. He could see how disappointed I was and to help cushion the blow he left me an open account at a boutique in the West End, and an American Express charge card number that I could use to buy whatever I wanted while he was away. He also bought me my first mobile phone. I had it all and I felt temporarily mollified.

To begin with it went all right. I stayed home and waited for him to return, and every evening he would ring for a chat. He always wanted to know where I was and who I was with. He never wanted me to go out with friends or see anyone. He'd suddenly become very possessive and jealous. I didn't like it, but I put it down to the fact that he was so far away. I told myself I should be flattered that he cared so much. But then the days turned into weeks and I grew tired of sitting around waiting for him. I had other men friends, like Mohammed, who were happy to take me out to clubs and parties and restaurants and I accepted their invitations, not caring how upset it would make him if he found out. Perhaps I even thought I could jolt him into action by giving him something to feel jealous about.

Then he rang to tell me his mother had died and I realised from his tone that things had changed. Like so many Arab men, I knew how much he revered his mother. I also knew she'd been increasing the pressure for him to marry his cousin because he'd told me so, and I felt that he might now feel he had to respect his mother's last wishes. I also guessed that losing a parent would focus his attention on the future and he would be thinking of the best ways to consolidate his own and his family's fortune. Marrying me was not likely to consolidate anyone's fortune. I was far more likely to spend it than increase it. I started to feel a stirring of disquiet at the way things were panning out.

My mother, probably worried that her daughter's chance of marrying into big money was in jeopardy, starting calling him and informing on me if I went out or saw another man.

Although he hated her, he didn't seem able to resist listening to her mischief making and believed everything she said. As the weeks went by I began to imagine what he was up to out there and became increasingly fed up with the way he was treating me, expecting me to stay in all the time just waiting for him to deign to come back to me. I started to think of ways to make some mischief of my own. I discovered that I could use his charge card in shops other than the boutique. It worked in jewellery stores and in car showrooms. With mail order I seemed to be able to order anything I wanted and my credit was never questioned. I became more imaginative and bought a cutlery set from David Morris for £45,000, sending it out to Saudi Arabia with my name and his engraved on it as 'Mr and Mrs'.

They had no qualms about serving me in David Morris because we'd been in together before he left and he'd bought us both £8,000 diamond rings with our names engraved inside. They'd assumed we were a couple, just as I had. It felt like I was getting some revenge on him for being away for so long and treating me like a possession, just putting me in a cupboard until he was ready to come back and play with me again.

Alarm bells must eventually have started going off at American Express because they sent their fraud squad round to visit me. Nice men who knocked on the door and asked politely if they could come in and discuss a few things. They wanted to know why I'd been using his card. They seemed more nervous of me than I was of them. I guess they shouldn't have allowed the debts to get so high before checking them and they were worried they might have to foot the bill if it turned out I wasn't authorised to run up that much debt.

'He's my husband,' I lied when they questioned my right to use the card with impunity. 'We had an Islamic marriage.'

There was nothing they could say. How could they prove it one way or another? They left the house looking even more worried than when they arrived.

Eventually my conscience got the better of me and I thought I'd better own up before someone else informed him. He'd gone from Saudi to Egypt for some reason and I rang him at the number he'd given me. My sister, Sandra, was sitting with me. I was sweating, not knowing how this was going to turn out. I had a feeling I was now going to have to pay a price for my mischief making.

'Listen,' I said, 'I've been using your credit card a bit.'

'OK,' he laughed. 'How much have you spent?'

'Seven or eight,' I said.

'Thousand?'

'You'd better phone them up and check,' I said. 'I think I've spent about £750,000.'

He took the news pretty well considering, but I never heard from him again. No one ever came to get back any of the things I'd bought and no one tried to get me to pay up for them. It simply went completely silent. I later heard that he'd married his older cousin. I saw a picture of her and she was surprisingly ugly. He was no oil painting himself but he could have done better than that. I guess there were financial implications to the marriage that no one outside the family would ever know about. I expect I would have made a terrible wife for him. I'm sure he needed someone who knew how to deal diplomatically with both family matters and business contacts, rather than someone with a dangerous habit of saying whatever she thinks. I dare say she never gives him any trouble and I would have given him a lot. But it might have been fun for a while. Perhaps he, like Karim and Ahmed, had a lucky escape.

I sold the house in Bushey and moved down to the centre of London, renting myself a flat in a nice portered block in Maida Vale. It had been another adventure and had taught me a lot about myself, not all of it good. It had also given me another insight into the way Arab men lived in the cosmopolitan modern world.

CHAPTER SIX

Becoming a Mother

AFTER THESE FALSE starts I did finally get married a few years later in Cyprus to a man called Theo. As with Ahmed, we met in a hotel when I was on holiday on the island with a friend. He fell in love with me straight away. What can I say? I was pretty in those days, and men fall in love easily with pretty young faces. That is the cruelty of the human condition. We fall in love and marry for reasons of the moment and then everything changes.

I liked him a lot and there was a pleasant simplicity to his life in Cyprus, which seemed appealing. There wasn't the extended family atmosphere that had surrounded the other men I'd been involved with, since Theo was an only child. But his mother, Flora, was a lovely, warm, welcoming woman. She was short and stocky and no-nonsense, which I liked after all the years of listening to my own mother's endless rubbish. Flora liked nothing better than to take her little dog for a walk along the beach or to cook a family meal. Whenever she was in the house she was always wearing her pinafore and busying herself with homely chores. Theo's dad was also a kind, sweet-natured, unpretentious man. It was a nice romance and then the holiday came to an end and, had it been left to me, I doubt if we would have seen each other again. Theo, however, had other ideas.

When I got back to England at the end of the holiday he was phoning me every day. His calls were not unwelcome but I still hadn't really thought of him as a potential partner for life. He was another wealthy man, half Cypriot and half Saudi, but, more importantly, he was kinder to me than anyone had ever been before. He just let me get on with doing my own thing. He wasn't jealous or possessive and he didn't try to change me. He was gentle, understanding and accepting. I was so grateful to him for that that in the following months I convinced myself I could marry him and live with him for the rest of my life. I had qualms, of course, just as I'd had with all the others, and I went back to Cyprus several times to be with him, to get to know him better and to try to work out what my true feelings were before I finally made up my mind. I probably would have sat on the fence forever, as I had before, but I fell pregnant during one of these visits and that put things into a different perspective.

Once that had happened and the maternal, nesting hormones had started to work, I realised I was quite happy with the idea of marrying him and moving out to the island permanently. Now that I was going to have a baby I didn't have any doubts about it being the right thing to do. In fact it seemed like a wonderful idea. I'd always liked the idea of becoming a mother. I wanted to do it all so differently to the way my own mother had and to build relationships with my children that I had never had with my parents. I also convinced myself that I liked the idea of bringing up a family in the peaceful, relaxed atmosphere of Cyprus.

The wedding was to be a civil service in the town of Paphos, since there was no big family on either side pressing for a giant celebration, and I felt nervous about committing myself to another potential fiasco in a huge white dress. At the time of the wedding I felt great: certain that I was doing the right thing. Afterwards I still loved the idea of being a mother but, as quickly as I'd fallen in love with Theo, I realised I'd fallen out of love once the vows had been exchanged and our future life together started to take shape. The idea of spending the rest of my life with one person suddenly terrified me and I became desperate to escape before it was too late. The island, which had seemed so peaceful and relaxed for short visits, suddenly felt restrictive and dull.

Flora, who lived a 20-minute drive away from our house, was just as wonderful and steady a mother-in-law as I had thought she would be and I was grateful to her for that. When my mother came out to visit us, however, it was obvious that the two of them would never see eye to eye about anything. I could almost feel the contempt oozing from the normally cheery and easy-going Flora as my mother turned everything around to make herself the centre of attention, going out to clubs at night and returning in the company of a number of unsuitable young Palestinian men. I think Flora thought it would have been more suitable if she had come out with my father to meet her daughter's new in-laws, and it wasn't hard to see her point.

Once my mother had gone and I had calmed down, my doubts about my future with Theo grew deeper. The bulge in my stomach was growing visibly and I became convinced that I had to get away before the birth because once he or she had arrived it would be doubly difficult to escape. There was also the danger that once the baby was born Theo would fight to hold on to it and I already knew that nothing would ever induce me to leave a child of mine behind. There would be a terrible battle and everyone would get hurt in the fallout, including the child.

It was the process of becoming a mother myself that first showed me how crucial the bond is between mothers and their offspring. I was then, and still am, convinced that small children should always be with their mothers rather than their fathers, unless there are exceptional circumstances. Relationships between couples go wrong for a million different reasons, as even my short history with men at that time would attest, but the mother and child bond is eternal and should be unbreakable in all but the rarest cases. I would soon have to put my principles to the test in the most heartbreaking of ways.

On the surface everything seemed perfect. After the

wedding we moved into the most beautiful house beside an orange orchard. It was so lovely it was like living in a fairytale. I even had a maid from Sri Lanka called Anna, who became my closest friend and confidante as I tried to get used to my new, tranquil, idyllic life. But inside my head and my heart it wasn't working. Although my lifestyle was comfortable and Theo was a kind husband, I felt trapped and desperate to escape. Because Theo was an only child there weren't many relatives around, only his mother and father, and I didn't have any friends of my own out there. So most days, when Theo was out working or down in the village, Anna and I were on our own in the house and I was lumbering around, hot and bored and heavy with child. No one dropped by unexpectedly for coffee. There was no one to cook meals for, or to swap gossip with. There were only the endless hours of peace and tranquillity.

I could see my whole life stretching out before me in exactly the same pattern: years and years of gazing out at the same perfect views and sitting in the same comfortable rooms. No doubt I would have more children, and that would be wonderful, but it couldn't be the only stimulation in my life. I panicked and began to plan my escape, with Anna as my accomplice. I couldn't talk to Theo about how I felt because I knew it was illogical and would be impossible to explain. How could I justify marrying him and then planning to abandon him within a few months?

I had to act quickly and decisively otherwise I would become too pregnant for the airlines to be willing to carry me. On the day I finally decided to go I rang a local shipping company and got them to come and empty the house of all my possessions, filling a container and putting it into storage under my name. They came with remarkable speed and I chivvied and hurried them through the work, desperate to be away from the house before Theo returned. As the container rumbled away through the orange trees Anna and I jumped into a waiting taxi and sped to the airport. We caught the three o'clock flight out of Cyprus that afternoon and I returned to England to give birth to Marlon, my first son. Anna stayed with me as a friend to help in any way she could. I still had the flat in Maida Vale to go back to and it was a relief to exchange the constant sunshine and peace of the orange grove for the busy streets of north-west London, and for the skies that were more often grey than blue. It was as if my extended holiday had finally come to an end. I had made exactly the same mistake as so many young Arab men do when they first come to the West, and now there was bound to be a terrible price to pay for Theo, Marlon and me.

Theo was amazingly sweet and forgiving about being abandoned so unexpectedly. He didn't panic as I think most people would have done. I'd expected him to rant and rave and threaten me with dire consequences if I didn't return to him immediately, but he remained calm and understanding and just kept trying to persuade me that I wasn't giving the marriage enough of a chance; that I should come back out to Cyprus and that we could move house if I wanted. Many of his arguments were very persuasive and maturely thought through. He assured me I would soon make a circle of friends on the island, particularly once Marlon was socialising with other kids and I was meeting their mothers, and that my life would get easier once I'd given it a chance. He was willing to do anything he could to make the life more tempting for me. I told him I'd think about it and I meant it. When I listened to him I wasn't at all sure that I did want to give up on the marriage. I certainly didn't want to make Marlon the product of a broken marriage just on a whim, if that was what it turned out to be.

Once I'd recovered from the birth and was getting into the routine of caring for a baby I decided that Theo might be right and that I should give married life another go. Anna, Marlon and I went back and forth to Cyprus a few times and Theo was always nice to me when I was there, never trying to stop me from returning to London when I felt like it. I insisted on keeping on the flat in Maida Vale, which I thought of as being as much my home as the villa among the orange trees. Knowing that I had that avenue of escape open to me whenever I wanted kept the feelings of panic at bay. In the good moments I thought perhaps I would be able to settle down and create a family unit in Cyprus, perhaps have some more children, but when it actually came to it I couldn't do it.

I allowed myself to be convinced that Marlon should be enrolled at a nursery school on the island. As soon as he started there, however, I wasn't able to come and go from London as I pleased and I felt trapped once more. With my little boy out of the house in the mornings I was alone again with Anna, restless and discontented, feeling new stirrings of panic. Theo had been resolutely patient and understanding and must have felt that, now Marlon was in school, he was finally safe; that I'd accepted my new life and was willing to stay, but I became increasingly certain that I was going to have to end it once and for all. I now regretted coming back from London at all because all I had done was extend the agony for all of us. Theo had now bonded with his son and would feel the loss more keenly if we left him, but that wasn't a strong enough reason to deter me from what I was planning to do. I knew I would feel much more guilty if I took Marlon away from his father now than if I had just stayed in London and the two of them had not got to know each other so well. But that wasn't a good enough reason to make a decision that would affect the rest of our lives either.

I can understand exactly why so many Arab fathers decide they can't stand to live with their Western partners any longer, because I have experienced that feeling of being trapped in the wrong place myself. I would never blame them for deciding to return to their home countries and familiar cultures. To be an alien every day of your life, even in your own home, is a tremendous strain on top of all the other strains of being a young parent. My only criticism of the men who make the same decision that I did is when they take the children with them with no thought of the bond they're breaking between the kids and their mothers. I've hurt a lot of people in my life, I'm painfully aware of that, but I've never knowingly hurt my children.

When I finally told him I couldn't stay in Cyprus and didn't want to live with him any more, Theo tried as hard as he possibly could to persuade me to change my mind. When it became obvious that I'd made my decision he argued that Marlon should stay in Cyprus with him because he was settled and happy, but I knew Marlon wouldn't be happy for long if I left. However wonderful Flora might be as a grandmother, she could not be a substitute mother for a small boy. It must have been awful for Theo, knowing that I was itching to leave him and that when I went he would lose Marlon as well. I could tell it was breaking his heart and I held off for as long as I could, but I knew I would go mad if I didn't get out. I didn't want to end up as bitter and disappointed as my mother had been in her marriage because I knew what misery that could bring to a whole family.

On the day I finally decided to leave I took Marlon out of school at 10 o'clock in the morning, just like the many fathers in England that I would hear about in coming years. I felt I had to do it in secret because I didn't want to risk Theo causing a scene in front of Marlon at the last moment. I didn't have any money of my own so I called my friend Mohammed in London and asked him to buy me tickets back to Heathrow, which he did. We flew out that afternoon, with the faithful Anna helping me. Mohammed came to the airport in England to meet us. This time I knew there would be no going back.

Theo must have caught the next flight to London when he discovered what had happened. He came straight to the flat in Maida Vale, brimming with an understandable fury, accusing me of playing dirty tricks on him and on the school. It was the first time he'd ever shouted at me or said anything horrible. By taking away everything he loved I'd finally driven this kind, placid man to lose his temper. He'd never shown me anything but gentleness and I was hurting him terribly. I had to explain yet again that I didn't love him any more, that it wasn't working out and that I didn't want to be with him. This time I could see that my words were finally sinking in. Maybe he just hadn't allowed himself to believe that it was over until that moment. Maybe he'd been clinging to the delusion that if he just waited long enough I would realise that life with him was what I wanted. At that moment he must have realised that his patience and kindness weren't going to triumph in the end, as he had hoped, and he looked devastated.

'You will never take my son,' he shouted in a final, futile show of bravado, his eyes full of tears.

'I will,' I replied.

'Over my dead body!'

'Maybe,' I said and my words must have shocked him because he fell silent. He must have realised at that moment that I wouldn't be changing my mind again, and that nothing he could do or say would make any difference to the situation. Marlon came into the room as we sat glowering at one another, and Theo looked at him with so much love I couldn't bear to watch and averted my eyes. I felt so sorry for the way things had turned out but I knew I couldn't do any different.

'I can't make you stay with me if you don't love me,' he said eventually, cuddling Marlon on his knee. 'I know I'll have to let you go. But it means I've lost my wife and my son. It is hard to know how to continue.'

I have great admiration for the way in which he came to accept the situation that day and we've remained good friends ever since. He never did anything nasty to me, even after I'd made him so unhappy. He's never tried to separate me from Marlon and he's always been totally supportive of his son.

I've never believed that all men are inferior parents to women. In some cases they may even be better parents than the mothers. Just occasionally I know a child is better off with its father than its mother, particularly if the child is a little older. But these cases are the minority. In most cases I can see that both sides have an equal amount of love for the children and the tabloid expression 'tug of love' is horribly true.

It's easy to see how the tug-of-love situations arise. When young men from good Arab backgrounds travel abroad to study or work they're overawed by the women they meet. They're used to women being protected by their families from the age of twelve. If they mess around with a girl they know they'll have to face the wrath of her father and brothers and every other male member of her family. But when they come to a country like England they see girls wearing skimpy clothes, and newspapers and magazines openly displaying naked flesh. They discover that it's even possible to sleep with girls and no one will be angry with them. In such a different world they often lose their heads. Any wisdom or judgement that they might have exercised in the calmer, more sedate worlds they have come from disappears. Away from their roots and without their family elders to advise them they sometimes make appalling decisions.

Often the women they meet in clubs and pubs are not of the same social standing as the men's own families, but because of the culture gap the men don't realise the significance of this until the children, which have resulted from the union, get to an age where the fathers start wanting to make some decisions regarding their future. Then the differences between the men and the women they have chosen really begin to show, and that is when most of the abductions from the West by fathers take place.

In most cases the fact that the men have different ideas about how to bring up the children is irrelevant; the women are perfectly good mothers and have every right to bring up their children as they see fit. In some cases, however, the women really aren't good mothers and the men are acting in the best interests of the children when they take them back to their own countries and to the care of their servants or female relatives.

When I first starting rescuing children for the women who asked for my help I didn't realise this fact. I saw things as being much more black and white; the women were the goodies and the men were the baddies. Because I couldn't imagine being separated from my children myself, I thought all women must be in the same boat. I assumed that all men who took children away from their mothers were acting in the children's worst interests and that the children should always be restored to their mothers without question.

The fact that things are not always as straightforward as they at first seem was brought home to me on a trip to Egypt, which I undertook for a woman who asked me to rescue her little boy for her.

There must have been something about the woman that I wasn't comfortable with from the beginning because I decided to undertake the trip to Cairo on my own, when I would normally, ever since the abortive trip to Morocco without Debbie, have the mother of the child with me. Like Debbie, she said she could only afford to pay for one ticket, and I accepted that without argument, even though I didn't believe in her case it was true. Usually in that situation, if I'd truly thought she couldn't afford it, I would have found a way to raise the money for the other fare myself. Something inside my head warned me that I needed to assess the situation by myself before I involved her. The boy in question was 12 years old, much older than I was used to dealing with, so I felt confident I could reason with him and persuade him to come with me, even if his mother wasn't there, if he was unhappy with his father.

I had a driver in Cairo who'd been very helpful to me on earlier missions and we'd become friendly. Knowing that I was on a very tight budget he offered me a bed in the spare room of his family home, which was a kind and welcome gesture. Not only are hotels expensive, they're soulless places to stay in, particularly when you're travelling alone. As I grew to know more people these sorts of invitations became more common when I was on missions. They nearly always came from people who lived in simple accommodation and had little money, but who were happy to share whatever they had with someone who they felt was genuinely trying to right some of the wrongs in the world. They were usually family apartments in suburbs and someone in the family often had to give up their room and their bed for me. I would always protest that I was happy on a sofa, or even the floor, but they would never listen. It is my experience that everyone in that part of the world wants to be as good a host as possible, however humble their circumstances might be.

The next day we found the house where the boy was living with his father and grandmother and other relatives. We watched their comings and goings for a while, just as I'd done at least half a dozen times by then. I wanted to familiarise myself with the main members of the family and their roles in the boy's life. He was too big for me to snatch him off the street; I was going to have to find a way to get close enough to talk to him, to explain that his mother missed him and wanted him back and that, if he was willing, I could help him to get to her. Alternatively, the first stage might be to negotiate for the mother to have access visits, but I couldn't decide that until I'd found out more about the true situation. I needed to find a way to win the family's trust.

His mother had told me a certain amount about their routine in Cairo, which she said she'd learned from letters her son had sent her in the early days of their separation. One of the things they did each week was go to a club to watch a show and eat a meal. I decided that the club might offer a way for me to stage a casual meeting, where I would be able to gauge the family situation and perhaps make some sort of contact. These types of clubs are wonderful places for anyone to visit, a sort of Egyptian version of British variety shows, with singers, magicians, comedians and other acts performing for diners. Sometimes they're held in open-air venues, where the audience is in grave danger of having their ankles bitten off by the mosquitoes hiding in the grass, but this venue was enclosed.

The driver and I arrived outside the club in the early evening. We parked across the street and watched for the car that we'd seen coming and going from the house during the day. The venue was just opening for the evening and the first guests were trickling in under the watchful eyes of the door staff. The streets were busy with evening trade as people emerged from their afternoon slumbers into the muggy evening air and there was no danger we would be spotted by anyone in the crowd.

The family's car drew up outside the door about an hour later. The boy, along with his grandmother and two other female relatives, got out and walked into the club. The driver and I waited a couple more minutes to give them time to get inside, and then followed behind, looking for all the world like a couple on a pleasant night out together.

The door staff didn't give us a second look; just two more punters to be seated, entertained and fed. We made our way in. The place was dark, crowded and full of noisy chatter. For a moment I couldn't make out where the family had got to. There was an expectant buzz as people waited for the entertainment to start, gossiped and ordered food and drink. Air conditioning made the atmosphere more comfortable than outside and drinks clinked with ice as the rushed waiters transferred them from trays to tables. A senior waiter tried to show us to a table but I sent him away. I wanted to be sure I was near to the family in order to observe them, overhear the way they talked to one another and possibly even strike up a conversation.

As my eyes grew accustomed to the gloom I saw them being settled round a table near to the front of the stage. The grandmother was making a fuss of the boy, ensuring he got what he wanted from the waiter who was serving them. They were absorbed in their own talk and not taking any notice of anyone else. I spotted another empty table just behind them and the driver and I pushed our way over to it, ignoring any waiters who tried to direct us to other parts of the room. Other people were heading in the same direction but none of them had the same determination as me. With the help of my elbows I managed to plant myself on a seat just behind the boy, close enough that I could overhear what he and his grandmother were saying to one another. I could see that he was very comfortable with the old woman and she seemed to be lavishing a lot of attention on him.

He was a good-looking boy with large, peaceful brown eyes and a ready smile for anyone who spoke to him. I felt an uneasy stirring inside. His mother hadn't struck me as being a particularly warm or loving person, and I doubted if she would have been treating her son as well as his grandmother was. He didn't look remotely uncomfortable or unhappy. This wasn't the picture that his mother had painted for me back in London.

She'd told me of phone calls when he'd sobbed down the line to her that he wanted to come home and that they were being cruel to him. She talked of letters smuggled out with tales of hardship and ill treatment. I couldn't imagine this well-fed, mollycoddled and cheerful young man doing anything like that. But even if his mother had misled me and exaggerated for the sake of making her point, that didn't mean she should be denied access to her son. She had a right to talk to him on a regular basis, if nothing else.

After a few minutes I managed to find an excuse to speak to the grandmother, asking her some question about the food she had ordered, and she seemed happy to engage me in conversation. She was a very open, friendly woman. She asked where I was from and I told her I was from England.

'My mummy's English,' the boy chipped in, and his grandmother stroked his hair affectionately.

'So where is your mummy tonight?' I asked innocently.

'She's back in England,' he said. 'I live with my daddy in Cairo.'

'You must miss your mummy' I said.

'No,' he shook his head. 'I like being here with my daddy.'

'You're just saying that,' I teased, 'because you love your grandmother a lot. You must miss your mummy a little.'

'No' he insisted, 'my mummy was bad to me. I like it here.'

'Oh, I'm sure you don't mean that,' I protested, wondering if it was possible he'd been brainwashed into thinking bad things about his mother, although I had a horrible feeling he was probably telling the truth.

'Look at this.' His grandmother pulled up the boy's sleeve and I saw the unmistakable marks left by old cigarette burns. 'She did that – to her own son. She's a bad woman.'

'I don't ever want to see her again,' he said, and I nodded my understanding.

There was no point in continuing to cross-examine him. It all seemed obvious to me now that I thought about it. We continued talking through the meal and during the quiet moments of the show, and by the end I knew that they were good, honest people. The boy's father had made a misjudgement in marrying the mother while in England but he was obviously doing his best to rectify the mistake for his son. Even if I hadn't believed them I could never have forced the boy to come with me against his will. I didn't even feel inclined to show my hand and ask if it would be possible for the mother to have reasonable access. I didn't want to bring unhappiness and discord into the lives of such a nice family, stirring up ugly memories for the boy. It seemed to me he was old enough and mature enough to make his own decisions now. If he didn't want anything more to do with a mother who had deliberately hurt him, then who was I to interfere?

That night I summoned all my courage and rang the mother in England to tell her I wasn't bringing her boy back to her. She went mad, screaming abuse down the line and accusing me of cheating her, reminding me she'd paid for my fare.

'I'll give you the fare money back,' I said. 'But I'm not bringing the boy back to you.'

I returned home empty handed. True to my word, rather

than live with the ill feeling, I reimbursed her every penny she'd provided and bore the cost of the trip myself. I didn't want anyone going around saying that I was in it for the money or that I was cheating people. There were enough charlatans out there in the marketplace doing that to these poor women. I couldn't stop myself feeling sorry for her because, even if it was her own fault and even if she had inflicted terrible pain on the boy in the past, she'd still lost her child and that's a terrible burden for anyone to bear, especially a mother.

The driver in Cairo isn't the only person who has shown me kindness and hospitality since I've been going to the Middle East and Northern Africa to look for children. Over the years I've built up something of a support network in the area. I have drivers in most of the countries now, all of whom I've kept in touch with after getting home and who I trust completely; men who know what I do and believe it's right that children should be allowed to stay with their mothers. I also have government and diplomatic officials I can go to sometimes for advice and help, and I've learned how to talk to them in order to get the information I need. The women that I help have none of this experience, which means they don't know where to start on their own. Sometimes I can find out where a child is at school by telephoning from England, which makes the planning much easier. It's amazing how much information people will give you over the phone, even senior government people.

It's also amazing how many men are willing to help me in my missions. One of the most prominent is Mohammed Al Fayed, the owner of Harrods and father of Dodi who, tragically, died with Princess Diana. He's been endlessly criticised by the media and by the Establishment for his outspoken views, but I've always found him generous and helpful. I first heard his name in this context when I was watching a woman on television who'd lost her two children to an Egyptian father. She was pleading from the television screen for Al Fayed to help her. I rang the television studios and left my name at the green room, telling her to ring me if she thought I could help. A few days later her mother called me. She told me her daughter lived in the UK but didn't have the money to travel south.

'She really wants you to help her,' the mother told me. 'She's at the end of her tether and you're the only hope left to her.'

I sent her the rail fare and arranged to meet her when she got to London. She stayed with us for three months while we worked out what to do for her. It wasn't easy having another woman in the house all day and every day, but she had nowhere else to go and I hadn't the heart to say no.

I thought that her idea of asking Mohammed Al Fayed, probably the most prominent Egyptian in the country, for help was good and that we should get in touch with him personally. It seemed unlikely he would have been watching morning television and heard her plea the first time. So I rang Harrods and was put through to his assistant. I explained the situation to her and asked if Mr Al Fayed would be willing to meet the mother if I brought her along to his office. The woman said she would ask and get back to me. Later the same day she rang to say that he would be happy to meet us. We went to see him together and I explained how I'd helped other women to get their children back and how I thought this lady was a worthy cause, but that she didn't have enough money for the fare to Cairo.

'So, you will go out with this lady and help her get her children back?' he asked once he'd listened to everything we had to say.

'Yes,' I replied, 'but I don't want paying for it, we just need enough for our air fares and any expenses we have to incur when we get there.'

He agreed to everything, without a second thought. He flew us out and booked us rooms at the very luxurious Cairo Hilton. Nothing was too much trouble. But then things began to go wrong. As soon as we arrived in Egypt my travelling companion made contact with the father of her children without asking me first. When I found out I couldn't believe it. We now had no element of surprise on our side, the father knew we were in the country and almost certainly guessed that we were planning to get to the children. If there had been any chance of getting close to them before, it had now vanished. The father then came to the hotel to see us. I asked him if my friend could see her children but he categorically forbade it. He didn't seem willing to even talk about the matter rationally. I couldn't see how we could move forward from this position and I was puzzled by the way the woman was behaving. She didn't seem as keen to see the children as she had been when we were in England. She appeared more interested in being with her estranged husband than anything else.

As he was leaving the hotel after our first meeting, I took the father to one side and asked if I could come and talk to his family on my own. I thought I stood a better chance without her there. To my surprise he agreed and I was taken to meet the children's grandfather. In the Arab culture the elders in most families have great influence. Everyone is brought up to respect their mothers and fathers and as long as the grandfathers are alive they're seen as the heads of the families, even if their sons are middle aged and independently successful. It provides a very stable base to their society and one that I believe families in the West would often do well to follow.

It seemed that I was going to have to negotiate with both generations. When I arrived at the meeting I was surprised by how pleasant they were to me. They didn't seem to see me as the enemy in any way. It was as if they thought there was something I could do to help them. I was invited to sit down with great courtesy, given tea and treated like an honoured guest.

'We did not steal the children,' the grandfather said, once all the social preliminaries had been dispensed with. 'Their mother did not look after them well, it was not a good place for them to be brought up.'

'But she should still be able to see her children,' I argued. 'No matter what she's done, she should have the right to visit and talk to them.'

'Of course,' the old man said, apparently completely in agreement with everything I said. 'My son plans to bring them to the UK for a visit, but his visa has run out and he is waiting for it to be renewed. We do not intend to keep her from her children, but we must put their interests first.'

I was a little confused but I decided to press my advantage while everyone was being so friendly.

'But she's changed,' I assured them. 'She's been living at my house for the last few months and there was no problem with drink or drugs. I don't even think she's with the same man any more. I do believe that the children should be with their mother if it's at all possible. She loves them and she wants them back. Look how hard she's been working to get to them. Surely she deserves a second chance. Let the children go back to the UK and I will make sure that your son has as much access to them as he wants. You have my word.'

We talked on and on and the grandfather seemed to be warming to me. He later bought me a gold ring as a token of his thanks for everything I was trying to do for his grandchildren. Eventually he agreed to my suggestions.

'Very well,' he said. 'You have convinced us. Take the children back with their mother. We will give her another chance.'

I couldn't believe my luck. I had never had a family make such a radical U-turn just from talking to me. Although I was thrilled, I had an uneasy feeling that it was all too good to be true. I went back to the hotel and told the mother the good news.

'I'm not going back,' she announced. 'I'm staying here to help my husband fight for his visa.'

'No,' I almost screamed, 'you can't do that. He'll get his visa in time. Just take the children while they're willing to give them to you, otherwise they may change their minds again.'

But no matter what I said she was adamant. The whole thing had been about getting a visa for the father to get back to England. She only wanted the children if she could get him as well. She wouldn't leave Egypt without her husband. I came away from the meeting realising I'd made a mistake. I rang Mohammed Al Fayed in London and told him what I'd found out.

'Don't worry, Donya,' he said. 'You've done your best. Just get yourself out of Egypt and back to your own children.'

So I left the woman with her husband and flew home. Even though he'd been misled, Mohammed Al Fayed never held a grudge against me; he could see we'd both been mistaken. We've stayed in touch and when I asked if I could take twenty children from my children's school to Harrods for a visit he laid on the full VIP treatment for them. He's funded other mothers to go and visit their children in the Middle East whenever I've asked him.

I'd learned by then that there's a great deal of goodwill in the world for mothers who've been parted from their children, but now I had also learned that things are seldom as they seem at first glance. Mohammed Al Fayed was not the monster I had been led to believe he was, and the mother who had convinced me her children were the most important thing in her life proved to have a different agenda entirely. I felt I was growing in wisdom with every mission.

My greatest ally and support in all my missions has been my second husband, Mahmoud. We met soon after I returned to England from Cyprus with Marlon for the last time. He's an Iraqi and he was working in a restaurant on the Edgware Road, where many of the best Arab restaurants in London are located. We met in the most unusual way. I rang the restaurant one night to order a take-away, which a friend went to fetch. When it came back the order was wrong. I rang up to complain and Mahmoud took my call.

He says that he felt he just had to meet the woman behind the voice on the telephone, so he brought round the replacement order himself. He obviously decided he liked what he saw and we started dating. As we got to know one another I saw the way he was with Marlon. He seemed to genuinely care for him and watch over him, just as a father should, and Marlon seemed to be totally comfortable with him. I began to think I could do a lot worse than to marry him. He was a gentle man who I knew would never try to restrict me. I had my life in London already and he would fit in with that, not expecting me to go and live in some isolated place away from my friends and family. He would add to my life rather than change it.

Still a devout Muslim, I knew I wanted to marry a Muslim man, but it had to be someone I could trust, and someone who would help and support me in whatever I chose to do with my life, although at the time we got married neither of us dreamed of what I would be doing a few years later.

We had the big wedding I'd always wanted, right from the

days of my meringue dress in Tunisia. The actual ceremony was in Marylebone Registry Office but we hired an Italian restaurant at Marble Arch, on the corner of Hyde Park, for the reception. I had a beautiful, straight silk dress covered in pearls and we provided all the champagne that our guests could drink and allowed them to order whatever they chose from the menu. We were determined to launch our marriage with a bang.

My mother wouldn't come to the wedding because I'd asked my father to give me away and at that time they weren't speaking. Dad had retired by then and had replaced his aircraft obsession with a motorbike obsession, taking the bikes to pieces and rebuilding them with just the same mixture of skill and enthusiasm. He's a big, bearded Santa Claus of a man and Mahmoud took him out and bought him a suit for the occasion. I felt very proud of him.

More or less a year later I gave birth to Khalid, my second son. All my children were born by caesarean section and Khalid proved to be a bright and wonderful child, but his health was never good. He had problems with his stomach, which meant he needed constant care and attention. Both of us were willing to devote as much time to him as he needed, which involved a lot of stays in hospital over the coming years.

A year later our daughter Amira was born, a tiny, curly-haired angel, and then came Alla a year later, the cheekiest and loudest of the bunch. This time there were even more complications with the birth and for a while it looked as if I wasn't going to make it. There was an emergency hysterectomy, which meant Alla would be the last child I would have. Had things not gone wrong I suspect I would have gone on having a baby each year until I hit the menopause. I just think they are the most wonderful things on earth and I can't get enough of them.

The night before Alla was born I had said to Mahmoud that I thought I was going to die the following day. I don't know why I felt like that. He dismissed my fears as mere foolishness, but during the operation things did not go well and for a moment it looked as if I wouldn't pull through. The doctors suggested to Mahmoud that he might like to warn my other close relatives that they should come in to see me, as it might be their last chance to say goodbye. I can remember being in the bed in intensive care with my mother and Sandra and Mahmoud standing around me. I could hear what they were saying, but I felt too weary to communicate back, so I just lay there and listened. I can remember hearing my mother telling Mahmoud that he would have to ship my body out to Cyprus to be buried. She must have been trying to annoy him even as he stood by his wife's supposed deathbed.

Needless to say, I didn't die and Mahmoud and I continued bringing up our brood. We adored being parents so much we could hardly bear to be separated from the children. When the time came for them to start going to nursery school we were both keen for them to get good educations, but couldn't stand being parted from them for so long. We used to find that the hours of separation were too painful and would make up any reason we could to go down to the school and see them through the railings, running around in the playground. We kept trying to find excuses to drop into the school to see them, but the staff told us we couldn't and shooed us away. As they grew older and moved to the big school we still didn't like being away from them for such long hours, so I became a parent-governor. I stood for election and received 86 per cent of the vote, an achievement I was immensely proud of. I made sure I played an active role in the school, helping with the administration, which meant I could be on the premises all day if I wanted to, seeing my children whenever the urge took them or me.

When I met Mary at the bus stop in Queensway and started on my adventures Mahmoud was completely supportive. His patience and kind-heartedness were to be put to the test time and again in the coming years, but he has never failed me and for that he has my everlasting love, admiration and gratitude.

CHAPTER SEVEN

Out of Iraq

EVERY MISSION IS very different, which means that there are no golden rules on what to do. Every time I set off I know that I am going to have to make it up as we go along. Yussuf was six years old when I went to get him and he was part of my own family. That made it easier in some ways because we were all working on the same side and I wasn't having to fight against the father's family, but had we been caught the penalties would have been terrible because of the methods we used to smuggle him out of Iraq and into Britain.

Yussuf's mother, Ibital, is my husband Mahmoud's sister. She was living in England with her other son at the time this rescue was planned, but Yussuf was still in Iraq with his father. Eventually the whole family planned to come over, but it was taking a terribly long time to arrange the necessary visas and paperwork. For every extra year that they were delayed, Yussuf was unable to be with Ibital. As you will by now be aware, I strongly believe that any child that small should be with his mother the majority of the time, regardless of whether they have the right pieces of paper or official stamps. It is a simple matter of humanity. I have no patience with bureaucrats sitting in offices playing God and deciding who will go where and when. I know it's important to have laws governing the mass movement of people, but there should always be a way for small children to be quickly reunited with their mothers. Any enforced separation is likely to be traumatic for them, even if they are living with kind and loving people. They should not have to wait for some pen pusher they will never meet to get round to stamping the right form before they can feel their mother's arms around them once more, and have her tucking them into bed at night.

Like so many other desperate women, Ibital and her family had explored every possible avenue to get Yussuf over to Britain sooner. There were organisations which had offered to smuggle him and his father in via Holland, but they were told that would cost at least $10,000 and Yussuf's father had no chance of raising that sort of money. Even if he had there was no guarantee that the operation would be successful and there would have been no way of the family retaining any control over what happened to them in transit. Another way had to be found. Every time I saw her, Ibital was becoming increasingly distressed at being separated from her youngest son, even though she had his older brother in England with her.

'I'll bring him over for you,' I said brightly one day when we were all sitting around talking about the problem, my mouth working on automatic pilot just as it had when I first offered to help Mary. Once I said the words it seemed like an obvious solution. I'd done it for virtual strangers, why wouldn't I be able to do it for a close member of my own family?

'What about his papers?' Mahmoud said, playing devil's advocate as always. 'He doesn't have a British passport.'

'He can travel on Khalid's,' I said. 'They're roughly the same age.'

'Don't be ridiculous,' Mahmoud laughed, tousling his eldest son's fair hair affectionately. 'Khalid is blond and blue eyed, Yussuf is dark haired and brown eyed. You won't get away with that. Any half-awake official will spot the difference and you'll be in prison.'

'We can dye Yussuf's hair,' I said, as if it was the easiest thing in the world to make a full-blooded Iraqi boy look like a blond English boy.

'Don't you think a little Iraqi boy with dyed blond hair is going to look a bit conspicuous?' Mahmoud laughed again. I was beginning to get annoyed with all his objections. I was used to just wading in with rescues and worrying about the details later, but I always had to admit, grudgingly, that Mahmoud's doubts helped to focus my mind at the beginning of each mission, forcing me to justify my plans and assumptions and to abandon some of my more ludicrous ideas before it was too late and I was committed to a course that was an obvious folly.

'OK.' I fell silent for a moment, thinking. 'We could shave his head then. We could say he has cancer. That'll get the sympathy of any officials who start sniffing around. They aren't going to want to upset a small child who's undergoing chemotherapy with too many questions, are they?'

'What about his eyes?' Mahmoud asked after a few moments' thought. I could see that I was winning him over to the idea slowly.

'He'll just have to keep them shut,' I said.

'How are you going to persuade a six-year-old boy to keep his eyes shut for six hours or however long the journey takes?' he asked, a little too triumphantly for my taste.

I had to admit that was a good point. I knew from experience of my own children how hard it was to get them to even sit still on a long journey, let alone keep their eyes shut and pretend to be asleep.

'We'll have to sedate him,' I said eventually. 'A couple of Valium should do the trick. As long as he has his eyes are shut at the moments when we're going through passport control at each end it'll be all right.'

Mahmoud threw his hands up as if he despaired of me, but he didn't put forward any more arguments. I guess he could see that I was going to do it whatever objections he raised, and he wanted to see his sister reunited with Yussuf as much as I did.

Although I'd tried to make it sound easy, I was very nervous at the idea of sedating such a young child. What if I accidentally gave him an overdose and made him sick? I'd have to give him the minimum amount possible, which meant he would also have to be taught how to behave in the moments when he wasn't asleep. He would have to learn to call me 'Mummy' and to say that his name was Khalid if anyone asked. I'd need to go over to Iraq some time before the trip back in order to teach him how to behave like an English boy. The idea of visiting Mahmoud's family was growing on me and I decided to take my daughter, Amira, on the trip with me. She was three-and-a-half at the time and I thought it would be nice for her to meet some of her father's family, and I knew that they would be very excited to see her. It would also make me look less conspicuous if I had two children with me.

I bought return air tickets to Jordan for myself, Khalid and Amira, even though Khalid wouldn't be coming. A woman friend called Jane had volunteered to travel out to Jordan with me and then come back with me again when I had brought Yussuf across the border from Iraq. I've always found that people are very happy to help out when they know it's for children. She was going to visit her family in Lebanon while I was in Iraq. This would give me another pair of hands to help if I needed them on the two flights.

Then it was off to the Iraqi embassy to apply for visas. We also needed visas for Jordan because we would be flying back from there, having crossed the border out of Iraq, with Yussuf posing as Khalid.

The plan was now taking its final shape. We were going to go to Heathrow and check in for the flight to Jordan. I would then claim that Khalid had been taken ill and send him home with his father. Khalid had always had poor health and I didn't think it would be hard to convince an airline official that he was not well. Khalid and Mahmoud would then go back home while Amira and I flew to Jordan with Jane. I had to hope that I could get Khalid's passport stamped as we went into Jordan. He would then officially be in the country and it would not seem odd when the time came to fly Yussuf back on the same passport. If I didn't get Khalid's passport stamped on the way into Jordan, it was bound to raise suspicions on the way out. The plan was not foolproof, but it was the best I could do, and I found that I was often lucky when I went into things by the seat of my pants. I'm a great believer in following hunches and trusting to luck and fate.

We went down to Heathrow as a family and checked in, with Jane in tow. Then, miracle of miracles, Khalid actually complained of feeling ill as we stood at the desk. I couldn't have persuaded him to time it better if I'd tried. I pressed my hand to his forehead and it was burning hot. Somebody up there must have been watching over us that day. He could never have been as convincing if he'd been pretending; nor, for that matter, could I. I now felt a mixture of relief at the plan going so well and concern that my vulnerable second child was going down with something real at a time when I was going to be a long way away from him for several weeks. For a second I wondered if I should postpone the trip and go home with him, but by then I felt committed and there was no choice but to keep going with the plan.

'You'll have to cancel his return flight and buy him another ticket,' the man from the airline told me, as I anxiously watched Khalid cuddling up to Mahmoud.

'No, no, don't worry,' I said quickly, trying to be as casual as possible. 'My husband's flying out in a few days. He can bring the boy out with him when he's better and then we can use the return ticket to come back as planned.'

The man looked as if he was going to protest but by then there was a queue building up behind us and he was under pressure to get the plane loaded and off. He obviously didn't want to upset a mother with a sick child so he nodded his agreement and let us wander off.

I said goodbye to Mahmoud and Khalid, giving Khalid's hot forehead one last anxious feel and issuing all sorts of instructions to his father about what to do with him as soon as they got home. Mahmoud kissed me to shut me up, promising that Khalid would be in safe hands and telling me to enjoy the trip. I felt terrible as we went through to the flight side, as if I was abandoning my little boy. I decided I must put him out of my mind for the moment and concentrate on the challenge ahead. Jane was very sweet, assuring me that Mahmoud could deal with anything that came up, and Amira was a good distraction from my worries. But once I was on the flight I couldn't stop myself from worrying about what was going to happen when I tried to get into Jordan with one less child than I was supposed to be travelling with. I knew it was crucial to get Khalid's passport stamped, so I would have to trick the officials in some way into giving a stamp to a child who wasn't there. My brain went round and round the problem and the possible ways I could get away with it, but each plan depended on certain circumstances, which I could not guarantee. Eventually I realised I couldn't plan in any detail what I was going to do, I just had to trust that my luck would continue to hold. The thought didn't make for a restful flight.

By the time the plane landed I could hardly breathe from the stress. Amira kept tugging at my hand and asking me questions but I couldn't concentrate on the answers, my mind was too preoccupied by what lay ahead of us. Jane saw that I was under pressure and scooped Amira up to answer her incessant stream of questions, allowing me to focus on what I was doing. I had to get this right, or there was almost no chance I'd be able to get Yussuf back out of Jordan in two to three weeks' time.

We joined the trail of passengers making their way from the plane into the airport building. There the queue was dividing into two different channels for having our passports and visas checked. Amira and I joined one side and Jane went to the other one. The queue was probably moving reasonably fast but to me it seemed to take an age. As we shuffled closer to the official looking at the papers I started calling out.

'Khalid! Khalid! Come back here. We're near the front of the queue. Khalid!'

Amira was too tired and disinterested in what was going on by then to point out that we'd left her brother back at Heathrow, so there wasn't much point in shouting for him now. The desk we were approaching was high and the official on the other side was out of her eyeline, so she was concentrating on her own small world and ignoring whatever her mother was doing. I guess she's so used to hearing me shouting at one or other of them that it goes in one ear and out the other. By the time it came to our turn to have our papers studied I was giving a good impression of an angry and frustrated mother.

'Where's your son?' the man asked, looking at the papers.

'He's so naughty, that boy,' I said in Arabic. 'He's run off through there.'

I gestured at the other side of the barrier. 'Will you please send someone to chase after him and tell him off?'

'It's OK,' he smiled, 'no problem.'

He stamped the passports and ushered us through. I guess he was probably a father himself and knew all about the problems of travelling with small children.

I felt so pleased with myself. It was like a weight being lifted from my shoulders as we walked through to the other side. What a result! I was in and I had the stamped passport for Yussuf to travel home on. Now I could relax and enjoy myself with the family for a few days. I walked straight out of the terminal with Amira, leaving Jane to collect the luggage. I wanted to spend as little time as possible being scrutinised by any cameras there might be around the building, which could pick up on the fact that I only had one child with me. The police at the final gate didn't ask to see passports again and so we were through into the outside world within moments.

Jane came through a few minutes later with the bags. She was flying out to Lebanon the next day so she checked into her hotel, and I found a taxi driver who was willing to take Amira and me across to Iraq for a reasonable price. Jane and I planned to meet again in Amman when it was time to go home, so that she could help me with the two children and the luggage on the return journey.

Once we'd said goodbye to her I went back to find the taxi driver. I was anxious to get to our final destination now. It had already been a long journey for Amira and the stress had been very tiring for me. The driver headed straight for the border, only stopping for petrol and refreshments every few hours. He seemed to keep going on cigarettes. We bought cold drinks from roadside stalls. The few people we came across on our short stops were very friendly and wished us well on our journey east.

At one point we stopped to freshen up at a communal washing area. As I walked in with my little blonde angel trotting beside me the women, who'd been bent over the sinks, talking away to one another as they worked, all drew back to let us through, commenting to one another in Arabic about Amira's hair. When I answered them in their own language they all crowded round, thrilled to meet someone from England, petting Amira and chattering to us happily. It felt like we were attending a wedding in a public toilet.

Despite my tiredness and worry I was pleased to be back in the Middle East, with its familiar sights and smells and the friendly faces of the people in the streets. Children would wave as we went past in some of the more outlying settlements, sometimes running alongside the car for a few yards. I had some crisps and snacks in my bag in case Amira became peckish but neither of us were that hungry. I was so tired after all the tension and excitement that I found myself nodding off in the back of the car, occasionally jerked awake by a sudden blast of the car's horn or the crash of the wheels in a particularly deep pot-hole.

The journey to the border took 18 hours and Amira slept most of the way, cuddled up against me. The car was dirty and hot and smelled of cigarette smoke, but the driver did his best to be pleasant and make us comfortable. There was a limit to what he could do. It was really an endurance test. I put my Walkman headphones on and listened to Van Morrison tapes as the barren countryside sped by. For hours on end we saw nothing but desert and it occurred to me that if we broke down we could be stranded for hours before anyone found us. The driver didn't seem concerned, so I assumed he knew the car was in good working order.

Finally we arrived, and Mahmoud's mother met us at the border. We moved all our luggage from the taxi and paid the driver. I didn't need to produce Khalid's passport again for the officials, as he wouldn't need to appear again until I was back at Amman airport and heading for England. It seemed to me we didn't need to convince anyone that he had been in or out of Iraq. Although it was a sense of achievement to have got this far, we still had a long way to go. It was going to be another nine hours driving to get to the town of Mejef, where Mahmoud's family home was. I was really longing to get there now. The thought of stretching out full length on a bed to sleep was so tempting.

I'd met Mahmoud's mother in England a few times and we'd got on really well. The whole family had been so welcoming to me when I married Mahmoud, and it was a wonderful reunion at the border that day. They seemed as excited to see us as we were to see them. They were particularly thrilled to have Amira visiting them because she's the only girl in the whole family, all Mahmoud's brothers and sisters having had boys. Knowing how important her birth was to them, I'd given Amira the second name of Fatima, after my mother-in-law. Mahmoud's mother is one of the kindest people I've ever met and has been more of a mother to me than my own mother ever was.

Mahmoud's family are quite comfortably off by Iraqi standards and have a nice house with massive wooden doors and a big garden full of fruit trees. After nearly 36 hours of travelling it felt, quite literally, like reaching an oasis in the desert. To be able to stretch our legs and lie down on soft beds, after sitting up in aeroplanes and cars for so long, felt like heaven. To be able to sit down to a relaxed meal, rather than grabbing snacks as we went, was bliss. When we entered the house there was a big welcoming party waiting for us. I rang Mahmoud to tell him we'd arrived safely and to find out how Khalid was. Mahmoud put him on the phone and I could tell from his voice that he had fully recovered. It was a weight off my mind. In the long hours of the journey I'd often pictured him lying sick in bed and felt horribly guilty that I wasn't there to nurse him.

When I came off the phone we all exchanged gifts and

everyone doted on Amira, who played up to them all beautifully, enjoying being the centre of attention. Yussuf was excited that we'd arrived because he knew that we were there for him and that soon we were going to be taking him to England to see his mother.

Both he and I were going to have to work hard, because I now had 17 days in which to train him to behave like an English boy in order to fool the airport authorities at both ends of the journey home.

'While we're travelling,' I explained to him, 'I'm your mum and that's what you must call me. We must practise from today, so that you're used to saying it by the time we leave.

'Your name for the next few weeks is Khalid and that's what I'm going to be calling you, in case I make a mistake and call you Yussuf in front of someone. OK?'

He nodded very solemnly, but how could he possibly have understood? He'd probably never been outside his village, certainly never been through an international airport. How could he have any conception of what was going to happen and how important it was that neither of us slipped up?

'If you do everything right,' I told him, 'when we get to London and to your real mum, I'm going to buy you a big bike.'

I then had to teach him enough English words so that he would be able to respond if anyone spoke to him or asked him a question. At that stage he knew no English words at all. He was a quiet, reserved little boy and it was hard to know what was going on in his head. Because he'd been living with his father and his grandparents for so long he'd been very mollycoddled – they didn't even expect him to feed himself. I had to change that. I couldn't risk him needing a meal on the flight and not being able to use a knife and fork. That would immediately have attracted suspicion. So we did a crash course in how to eat like a little English boy. He was very keen to do whatever I asked, but he found it hard; both of us did.

The visit wasn't all work; I got to act like a tourist as well. Although I'd been to Iraq in the past I'd never visited this part of the country and they took me to see things I'd never seen before. I was amazed by what they showed me. We went to visit wonderful holy shrines and I was shocked by how much poverty I saw in the villages we drove through. In each settlement there seemed to be a cluster of rich men's houses and then there were the peasants all around who appeared to have been hit hard by the economic problems the country was experiencing. There seemed to be plenty of goods in the shops for the people who could afford them, but those people seemed to be very much in the minority. Many of the buildings looked as if they'd been there for thousands of years, with each generation adding to them as their families expanded. It had the feeling of a land that had grown organically, a million miles away from the clamour and shabby modernity in parts of some of the big cities in the region.

Mahmoud's late father, who had been a successful businessman and had left the family comfortably off, was buried in a grave about a 10-minute car ride from the house and we visited him to pay our respects. Mahmoud's other sisters lived in their own houses close to the grandparents in the same traditional style that I had first encountered with Karim's family. They all looked after one another, a close-knit community with roots stretching back down the generations, a million miles away from the transient community we lived amongst in London, where we often had no idea who our next-door neighbours were, let alone the people down the street.

There were bad things about life out there as well, of course. I had to get used to the cockroaches that scuttled across the floor whenever we came into rooms unexpectedly and crunched under our feet if we trod on them. There were also the tiny frogs that sang outside the house in the evening. Amira would go looking for them on the shaded lawn, screaming with a mixture of fear and delight as they sprang vertically from the grass, jumping higher than her head, seeming to deliberately tease her as they hopped away. She would run through them, shrieking all the way, and take refuge on the garden swing, watching them bouncing around her, eyes wide with horror.

It was August, the height of summer in one of the hottest places on earth. The temperature during the day was almost unbearable, baking everyone and everything to a standstill. The electricity would only come on for a couple of hours a day, so it was impossible to run air conditioning or fans; you just had to endure the heat by moving slowly to conserve your energy and staying in the shade as much as possible. During the hours of greatest heat a blanket of silence seemed to fall over everything, smothering the voices of birds, insects, animals and people alike. It was hard for Amira, who developed a nasty heat rash at the top of her legs.

Once the sun had gone down I'd sit out in the garden in the cool of the evening air and stare at the stars, which seemed so much brighter than in England, and think about my husband and sons back in London, wondering how they were getting on without us, trying to imagine what part of their daily routine they would be enjoying at that moment. It was so peaceful and the air was so clear it made you feel desperately alive after the enforced hibernation of the day. I felt very happy there, despite missing my family and being nervous about the journey to come. The people were so gentle and kind and non-judgemental. They all seemed to accept me arriving in their midst without question or suspicion.

Even the people we met casually in the souks were to keen talk to an English woman who'd married an Iraqi and spoke their language. Sometimes they just wanted to touch me, as if checking that I was real. It felt as if I'd travelled back in time, like I was living in the days when the Koran was written, holy times when men and their lives were less complicated and the rules were clearly understood. If it wasn't for the government, I thought at the time, and all the trouble that it was bringing down on the heads of its people, Iraq would be a wonderful country to live in, but no one can prosper under such an oppressive regime, particularly when large parts of the world are so intent on bringing that regime to its knees by making life for ordinary people as difficult as possible. And so Yussuf had to leave this wonderful country and follow his mother to England in order to be free.

Amira adored her grandmother. Fatima is a big woman and she would hide her little granddaughter under her capacious black robes when they went out, to guard her from the 'evil eye'. She said Amira was so pretty she was in danger and had to be hidden. Amira didn't care about the danger, she just loved the attention. For her the whole trip was no more than a holiday and a chance to be completely indulged. She knew nothing of the impending peril that was approaching as we prepared ourselves to smuggle her little cousin out of Iraq and into Britain.

By the time my 17 days were up I could see that, although Yussuf had tried his hardest to remember everything I'd told him, he still wasn't ready to pass himself off as a little English boy under anything approaching close scrutiny, and there was still the problem of him looking completely different from the description in Khalid's passport. We were going to have to resort to my first plan of changing his appearance and tranquillising him. I could see that Mahmoud had been right about my idea of dying his hair blonde; it would have looked completely false against his sun-darkened skin, and there would still have been the problem of his eyebrows and eyelashes and the dark fluffy down which grew on his arms.

Yussuf's father had managed to get visas for himself and Yussuf to cross the border into Jordan and he was going to travel up to Amman with us. That would make the boy more comfortable about the first leg of the journey and we decided not to do anything about altering his appearance until we were in Amman, so he could use his own passport to get out of Iraq. We hired a driver for the long trip back across the desert. I felt very sad leaving the people who I now thought of as my own family as much as Mahmoud's. It must have been hard for my mother-in-law to see both Yussuf and Amira waving goodbye from the back of the car, knowing that they were going to be travelling so far away from her. I could tell she'd really enjoyed her time with them and would miss them terribly. I watched from the car window as we drove away and she stood outside the house waving until we were out of sight. She must have wondered if she would ever see them again. I thought of Marlon's grandmother, Flora, alone in her little house in Cyprus, deprived of the chance to watch her grandson growing up because I'd been unable to make my life with her son, and felt a pang of sadness. So many people suffer such blows in their lives through no fault of their own. Although Flora and I do occasionally speak on the phone, and the conversation is always polite, I'm sure she must still hate me for what I did to her family. If I was her and some woman had taken away my beloved grandson, so that I never saw him again, I don't think I would be able to forgive her.

There were no problems on the drive up to Amman, just the same long hours of tedium and discomfort that we'd endured on the way down. Everything went smoothly at the border crossing between Iraq and Jordan. When we got to the city we put our minds seriously to the question of Yussuf's appearance. We were staying in the apartment of a friend of mine and there, the day before we were due to fly, we started transforming Yussuf into Khalid. We used a pair of electric clippers to take the bulk of the hair off and then we used a razor to get rid of the wisps that were left behind. It was so sad to see the thick, glossy black locks falling to the floor in clumps.

'We should collect them up and knit him a wig,' I joked as we sheared him bald. I could see that Yussuf was horrified by what we were doing to him and no amount of joking would help.

'Don't worry, Khalid,' I kept saying. 'It'll grow again in no time. And when we get to England I'll buy you a hat to keep your head warm.'

Just taking the hair off made a dramatic difference, but it also made him more noticeable. People would be staring at him, which meant that we had to deal with any other detail that might have given him away. His thick, dark eyebrows were the next things to fall victim to the dreaded buzz of the clippers. Then we had to shave off the dark hairs that were starting to create a film on his skinny little arms. Although they hardly showed up against the brown skin, they would be enough to give the game away if anyone looked closely enough. I knew that if we wanted it to look as if he had been having serious chemotherapy all this hair would have to go, plus he had to look like he'd been blond before the treatment started.

I felt terrible having to alter his appearance so much. He was such a handsome little boy and by the time I'd finished with him he looked like he'd just walked out of a concentration camp. The big dark eyes stared sadly out of the hairless little face, making me feel even more guilty, and even more aware that we'd have to make sure those eyes remained closed throughout as much of the trip as possible.

The official story from now on was that little Khalid was dying of leukaemia and was undergoing chemotherapy to try to prolong his life.

Our flight was due to leave at two o'clock in the morning and Jane was flying in from Lebanon to meet me at the apartment, so that she could help me getting through the airports at each end of the journey. If I was going to be tranquillising Yussuf one of us would have to carry him, while the other took care of the luggage and Amira. Carrying a six year-old as a dead weight for any length of time is no small task and I wouldn't have been able to manage him on my own without running the risk of drawing attention to myself.

My stomach was churning with the familiar sensation of fear mixed with adrenaline as we walked into the almost deserted night-time airport, feeling like a small party of refugees. I would have felt far less conspicuous if it had been the middle of the day with milling crowds of people to disappear amongst and overstretched officials trying to process everyone as fast as possible. I knew I was doing something highly illegal in both Jordan and Britain and I was terrified. If we got caught at that stage we would have been on our way to jail without any doubt at all. Travelling on false papers was a serious crime, but I was committed now; Yussuf's father had gone back to the family in

Iraq and there was no going back. Having shaved and drugged the poor boy, I could hardly chicken out now.

The bored and sleepy official who looked at our passports didn't pass them back immediately and stared hard at my face for a few moments. I averted my eyes, not wanting to appear confrontational, but at the same time anxious not to look furtive. It felt as if he was trying to drill through to my brain and read my thoughts, searching out my guilty secrets. He called over some colleagues, who didn't seem to have enough to do, and they all huddled over our papers, talking and shooting us sidelong glances, and then called us to one side. Jane had Yussuf in her arms, a baseball cap on his head and some dark glasses covering his eyes, which were too big for his face and kept slipping down his nose. He was fast asleep from the two Valium tablets we'd administered just before leaving the apartment, combined with the exhaustion of the trip so far. Jane hitched him up on her hip and his head lolled on her shoulder. I noticed a thin line of saliva had dribbled from the corner of his mouth on to her scarf, but I didn't bother to clean it up – it added to the illusion that he was sick.

I was proud of the effect we'd managed to achieve with him. I'd dressed him in Khalid's clothes and given him a *Star Wars* rucksack. He looked like an English boy on holiday. We'd even put the poor child in a nappy so that it wouldn't show if he wet himself while he was asleep.

'Why did your son not go to Iraq with you and your daughter?' One of the officials wanted to know, pointing at the stamps in the passports. I felt like my stomach was going to fall out of me. My skin grew clammy and I think I must have gripped Amira's hand painfully hard because she let out a little squeak of surprise.

I looked him straight in the eyes, mustering all my acting skills. 'My son is dying,' I said, gesturing towards the lolling head of Yussuf. 'He's got cancer. He only has a few months to live. I wanted to take him to the holy shrine in Iraq to say prayers for him to get well, but he wasn't strong enough to make the journey.'

It sounded such a sad story I felt tears coming to my eyes and there was a catch in my voice. I'd like to claim it was my superb acting skills but I think it was pure nerves, mixed with exhaustion.

'He stayed with friends here in Amman and we went on to say prayers on his behalf.'

I'd anticipated this question and lined up an alibi if necessary. The friend whose apartment we'd used to prepare Yussuf for his change of identity had said he was willing to say that Yussuf had stayed in Jordan with him while we went down to Iraq.

'OK.' The official handed back our papers, still looking doubtful. 'You go ahead.'

'Is there anywhere here where we could pray?' I asked.

'Yes,' he said in a softer voice, evidently touched by the sight of such a devout woman trying to do the best she could for her dying son, 'upstairs, you take him up.'

As we went up the stairs he was pointing to, eager to get somewhere where we would be out of sight of security cameras, we heard an announcement about our flight echoing around the quiet building. It had been delayed by three hours. My heart sank. The longer we were around the nearly empty terminal, the more likely it was Yussuf would wake up and the more likely we were to attract the attention of the authorities in some way. But there was nothing I could do. We would just have to grit our teeth and endure the tension.

I could see where the prayer room was, but I didn't want to go in there yet. If anyone asked I'd say we were going in later, once we'd rested. We found some chairs away from everyone else and sat down. Jane dropped Yussuf on to a seat with obvious relief. He was beginning to stir and make low moaning noises. The dark glasses had slipped right to the end of his nose, making him look like an inebriated ventriloquist's dummy.

'I think he's coming round,' I said.

'What are we going to do?' she asked as Yussuf's eyes fluttered open, startlingly dark brown in the hairless face.

'We'll have to give him another tablet,' I said.

'We can't,' she said, horrified. 'We'll kill him if we're not careful.'

'We don't have a choice. We have to keep him quiet for the next few hours. He's meant to be dying. If he starts running around the airport we're done for.'

Yussuf was mumbling something. I leaned close to catch his words.

'He says he needs to go to the toilet,' I said.

'Can't he just go in the nappy?' Jane suggested.

'If he does we could end up having to change it before he even gets on the flight, which would be bloody hard with a child his size.'

'I'll take him to the toilet,' Jane volunteered with a resigned sigh, hauling him back up on to her shoulder and carrying him off.

As she disappeared into the ladies a voice came over the loudspeaker system again, calling me back to passport control. I couldn't believe I'd heard it right. I listened intently, my heart thumping in my chest. The message was repeated and there was no doubt it was my name. Once again my stomach seemed to fall through the floor. I looked frantically at the toilet doors, but there was no sign of Jane. She would be at least a few minutes wrestling poor Yussuf in and out of his nappy. I couldn't wait for her. I didn't want to draw any more attention to myself than the announcement had already. It would be better if I went back down on my own anyway now that Yussuf was conscious.

As I walked down the stairs I felt like I was heading to my own execution. I imagined how the police would be waiting for me at the desk and how I would be whisked away in a police van and wouldn't see my children for years. I even thought about making a run for it, but I knew the idea was stupid; they'd get me before I even reached the door. I had Amira on my hip and she seemed so innocent and unconcerned by everything, just looking around at what was going on, asking questions and pointing to things. I imagined having to be parted from her if they arrested me, and not seeing her again until she was a grown-up schoolgirl if I received a prison sentence and I started to tremble.

When I reached the desk the officials were waiting for me. They didn't seem to have anything else to do. They beckoned me over. None of them were smiling, as if they deliberately wanted to intimidate me.

'Your papers!' one of the men demanded, holding out his hand for them.

I pulled them out of my bag, trying to balance Amira at the same time, and passed them over the desk. I noticed my hand was shaking. I was tempted to just confess everything and throw myself on their mercy in order to end the terrible suspense. Perhaps if I did that they would be more lenient and only put me in prison for a few months instead of a few years. I forced myself to keep quiet and hold my nerve for a bit longer, just in case it was a false alarm. My throat had gone dry and I wasn't sure I would be able to reply if they asked me a question. It was hard to breathe and I was afraid I was going to faint. I was worried I would drop Amira and forced myself to stand firm. The man took the papers from me and looked through them, nodding as if his suspicions were being confirmed, and showed them to his colleague. The other man looked at the papers and then up at me, his eyes accusing.

'You stayed three days longer than your visa,' he said. 'You have to pay a fee.'

A wave of relief swept through me, making me smile involuntarily. That was all it was. I'd overstayed my allotted time and owed them a few pounds. It wasn't much. I found the money in my bag and handed it over, trying not to show how eager I was to get away from the desk and back to Jane and Yussuf. I felt like I could breathe again, but my legs were still shaking. It was hard to climb the stairs and Amira kept wriggling in the crook of my arm, getting a second wind and wanting to be put down so she could run around. I sank back down into the seat next to Jane who had emerged from the toilet with a sleepy Yussuf and hadn't witnessed any of my drama. I explained what had happened and we huddled together quietly, hoping to be invisible until it was time to go out to our plane. Amira was now full of life and eager to involve Yussuf in her games. He smiled at her benignly as she tried to galvanise him into action.

Eventually, when our nerves were stretched to breaking point, our flight was called and we made our way out towards the plane. Every security procedure seemed to take twice as long as normal, as if we were caught in a slow-motion sequence in a film. I don't know if they were actually being particularly cautious on that flight, or whether it was just that I was so anxious to get going it seemed like every movement was taking an age. My stomach was turning over and I felt sick with fear as we made our way towards the gate, every hair on my head and body seemed to be standing on end. I could see from her eyes that Jane was equally panic-stricken. Yussuf, having had another Valium a few minutes earlier, had drifted back to sleep. The officials seemed to glower at us with particular ferocity as we went through the gate, but maybe it was just in my imagination. Maybe they always look like that but you don't notice when you have a clear conscience and you're concentrating your mind on getting to your flight. Finally, we were inside the aircraft, talking to the cabin crew, and Amira was settling herself cheerfully into her seat, lapping up the attention of the stewardesses and oblivious to the turmoil her mother's mind was in.

After what seemed like days, the doors of the plane were pulled shut, the engines roared into life and we trundled down the runway, for miles and miles and miles. Just when I felt sure we must have turned round and headed back towards the terminal because no runway could be this long, the wheels lifted off the tarmac and we were out of Jordan and on our way. But the ordeal wasn't over. It wasn't a through flight. We were going to have to change planes in Greece. If we'd simply been kidnapping a child from an Arab country we would have been in the clear on Greek soil, because we'd have been out of the jurisdiction of the father's home country, but Yussuf was actually travelling on a false passport, so we could easily be taken off the plane in Athens and possibly sent straight back to Jordan, or put into a Greek jail, which would probably not have been any better than a Jordanian one.

By the time the plane began to descend into Athens, Yussuf was waking up again. He'd managed to have something to eat and was obviously feeling a little livelier. I was relieved that we hadn't done him any permanent damage with the tablets, but nervous that he no longer looked like a sick child. I didn't dare risk sedating him again, wanting to save that up in case we needed it at Heathrow, so I put his cap and dark glasses on him again and told him to keep as quiet and still as possible. As we came off the plane uniformed airport staff hurried towards us, waving their arms and shouting. My heart missed several beats and I felt the blood draining down from my face. I fought the urge to grab the children and run for my life across the runway.

'Quickly, quickly, quickly,' they were shouting, 'your plane is waiting to go.'

The delay to our Jordan flight meant that the Greek plane was waiting on the tarmac to take off. We ran straight on and took off once more. The ground crew were all far too busy trying to hurry us up to take any notice of Yussuf and his passport. Now all we had to do was get past passport control in Britain.

'We could just leave him in the airport for his mother to come and get him,' I said to Jane as we mulled over the options open to us. I was feeling terrible and not sure my nerves were going to be up to going through the ordeal again. 'Or we could keep going and try to take him through on Khalid's passport. It's worked once so it might again.'

'They're likely to be tougher here than in Amman,' she said.

'I know,' I agreed. 'What do you think we should do?'

'If we leave him they'll still know it was us who brought him in because we checked in with him in Amman. At least this way there's a chance we'll get away with it. We have to keep it up.'

'But we've had so many lucky breaks already,' I argued. 'Our luck can't hold forever.'

'I don't think we have a choice.' She squeezed my hand. 'We're almost there. Don't lose your nerve now.'

I nodded and smiled back. I was very glad to have her there for moral support. I knew leaving Yussuf on his own wasn't really an option, but I just wanted the whole journey to be over and for Amira and me to be safely back home with the rest of our family. It had been a long and gruelling journey and my nerves were more frayed than they'd ever been before.

Yussuf was awake but subdued as we went through British passport control, wearing his dark glasses to cover his eyes. The officials glanced at him and looked away. Maybe they were embarrassed to stare at a child they could see was not well. They nodded us through. I wondered if it was a trap; if they were trying to lull me into a false sense of security in the hope that I would give myself away. I told myself I was being paranoid. As we got to the luggage reclaim area Yussuf started to whine. He must have known that we were nearly at the end of the journey and that he would soon be reunited with his mother and he was becoming impatient. I couldn't blame him, but I just needed him to hold on for a few more minutes. If he attracted attention now they'd call us back and we'd be done for. I was feeling so tired myself I could hardly stand. I tried to comfort him while Jane frantically searched for our bags on the carousel. There was no sign of them and there were several men in uniform moving towards us. Yussuf was starting to make a lot of noise, despite my attempts to calm him and people were looking in our direction.

He was saying something in Arabic and for some reason I couldn't understand. It was as if every word of the language had deserted my exhausted mind and I couldn't think what he was saying. Then I heard some of the words and realised he was asking for the toilet again. I took him quickly into the ladies to settle him down and to get away from prying eyes. Once he'd emptied his bladder he quietened down. I took him back out and the head of security came over to me, with two porters.

'Is everything all right, Madam?' he asked.

'No, it is not,' I said, deciding to take an aggressive stand in the hope of getting us out more quickly. I could hear my own voice as if it belonged to someone else and it sounded close to tears. 'My son has got cancer. He's really ill and they treated us so rudely on the aeroplane. He's been sick everywhere and now our luggage is delayed and he's having to wait when he should be home in bed.' Yussuf let out a loud moan as if on cue and I pressed his head to my shoulder to quieten and comfort him.

'Don't worry,' the man said, soothingly, 'we'll help you with the luggage. We'll take you through. What do your bags look like?'

I described our bags and they disappeared behind the scenes to look for them.

'They're going to take us through,' I told Jane out of the corner of my mouth.

'What happens if his mother's on the other side and he spots her and starts shouting her name?'

'Oh God!' It hadn't occurred to me. 'I did tell her not to come to the airport.'

'What if she couldn't bear to wait another moment? She hasn't seen him for 18 months, for God's sake!'

'Just pray,' I said, as the porters came back with trolleys containing our stuff and led us towards the exit.

As we came through into the main concourse I saw Mahmoud waiting for me with a huge bunch of flowers. There was no sign of Ibital and I sent up a prayer of thanks. Mahmoud had a driver with him. We left the airport looking like a happily reunited family and drove back to Maida Vale. I have never felt so drained in my life.

As we travelled along the motorway I got out my phone and dialled Ibital's number.

'I've got someone here who wants to talk to you,' I said when she answered, passing the phone over to Yussuf.

'Hello, Mummy,' he said in Arabic, and I wept as if my heart was breaking.

CHAPTER EIGHT

Narrow Escapes

HAVING CHILDREN and bringing them up is one of the most rewarding experiences life can offer, but it doesn't exactly set the pulse racing on a daily basis. Children like routine, they like to know what's going on around them all the time. For an adult mind that can be very wearing if you don't get a chance to do something else from time to time. I welcomed the opportunity to court a little danger and remind myself that I was still alive in every sense of the word, not just as someone else's mother. There were moments, of course, when I would have preferred to have a little less excitement, certainly at the time, but that is the point of adventures, the feeling of not being in control of what happens.

One of the most frightening countries to rescue children from is Turkey. It may be just because I remember those scenes in the film *Midnight Express* where the hero is caught smuggling drugs and confined to a Turkish prison, but I think it's more than that. The police out there seem to be more organised and more ruthless than in most of the other countries I've had dealings with. So when I go there on missions I always have a feeling that there's a greater likelihood of getting arrested, and I have some vivid pictures in my mind of what would be in store for me if I was.

The possibility of being caught and sent to prison is always with me on all the trips, but with some the likelihood of it happening has seemed greater than others. There also seemed a greater chance of a long sentence in some countries, where I suspected they would be eager to teach a stern lesson to any woman who was presumptuous enough to challenge the rules of men.

On one Turkish mission, I had to go to the tourist resort of Marmaris to try to find a seven-year-old girl for her mother. Just as in Morocco, it was like trying to find a needle in a haystack when I looked at all the small girls playing on the beaches and wandering around the town with their parents. Initially I went alone because the mother couldn't afford two tickets. I arrived at the resort and went down to the main beach, having booked into my hotel. I tried to explain to her that it hadn't worked for me before but she was so worried about the expenses that I agreed to go alone to pacify her. I remember the terrible sinking feeling as I saw the crowds and realised I would never be able to pick out the girl. I didn't give up immediately. I wandered around town for several days, sitting in cafés and watching, or walking up and down in the surf, barefoot and carrying my shoes, in the hope that I might see a face that looked like the out-of-date school photograph I was carting around with me, or hear a voice that would give away an English background.

There were so many false alarms, so many small girls who for a few minutes I was certain was the one I was looking for. I would hover near them for as long as I dared, watching them with their families and trying to work out if it was possible it was the child I was after. But they never were. There was always something that persuaded me I was going to have to keep looking: they would call a woman Mummy or speak such fluent Turkish that I didn't think they could be newly arrived in the country.

'It's no good,' I told the mother over the phone at the end of the third day of fruitless searching. 'You're going to have to come out to join me. I'll pay for your expenses.'

I think she was relieved to be able to join the search personally. It must have been hard for her, sitting in England, not knowing what was going on or what I was doing. She must have wondered if I was walking within inches of her lost child and just not spotting her. She arrived the next day and we started searching together. After five days we realised it wasn't going to work.

'They must have finished their holiday by now,' the mother said as we sat in our room, feeling depressed and wondering if we should give up. 'It's possible he's taken her back to Istanbul.'

She'd already tried to make contact with the girl and her father at his old home in the city and had had no luck, which was why we were trying to find them while they were on holiday. It did seem possible that having seen no sign of the mother for several months, the father might now be feeling more confident and would have brought his daughter back to his home.

We checked out of the Marmaris hotel the next day and headed for Istanbul. Now I really was nervous. It's always more dangerous in a big city, where there are more people to interfere with whatever you're trying to do, more police and better communications. If a child is snatched in a big city the police can be informed within minutes and they're usually sophisticated enough forces to be able to close down airports and seaports within an hour or so. But I was committed to the job now and couldn't let a few qualms stop me. I'd grown to like the mother a lot and I could tell that her affection and need for her daughter were genuine. I was prepared to stay with this one to the bitter end.

The father lived in an apartment block slightly away from the centre of the city. It was not a particularly nice area, but not a slum, just like the outskirts of hundreds of other cities around the world, I guess. I didn't bother to check into a hotel because I wanted to be sure the child was there before we incurred any more expense.

We hired a car and parked within sight of the entrance to the block, settling in for the usual waiting game. We needed to ascertain that the girl was there and then we had to work out what her daily routine was like in order to calculate the best moment to strike.

We'd only been sitting there a couple of hours when a group of children emerged from the building, apparently with no adult supervision.

'That's her!' the mother shouted, making the driver and me both jump out of our skins. She reached for the door handle and I grabbed her hand.

'Wait a second,' I said. 'Let's think this through. We need to check that there isn't anyone watching them.'

'OK.' She sat back in the seat with an obvious effort of willpower, unable to tear her eyes away from the sight of her daughter playing in the sunshine. 'How long do we wait then?'

'I don't know,' I admitted. 'I just need a second or two to gather my thoughts.'

We sat in a tense silence for a few minutes and then I made a decision. There didn't seem to be anyone watching and there might never be another opportunity this good.

'OK,' I said, 'you're right. Let's do it now. Walk over to her really casually so the other children aren't alarmed. We don't want them running off to their parents saying a strange woman is kidnapping their friend. Make sure they realise you're her mother. Then get her back into the car as quickly as possible. If anyone appears out of the building I'll come over and help you.'

She was out of the car so fast I felt the breeze from her scarf. I watched, poised for action if needed, as she walked across to the group. I saw her daughter look up, firstly with a puzzled expression on her face and then with a look of sheer joy. The other children stood back respectfully to watch as their friend embraced her mother, and then waved cheerfully as the two of them walked back to the car, hand in hand, chattering like nothing in the world was wrong.

'Come on, come on,' I muttered under my breath as they sauntered back towards us. I could see a group of adults coming round the corner of the building and wanted to be away from the scene before they reached the playing children. The driver started the engine. I could see he was watching them approach just as anxiously as I was.

Finally they were inside the car, the doors were shut and the driver was speeding away. I looked back at the people I'd seen; they'd reached the children and were talking to them. The children were pointing at us and the adults were looking, their palms flat above their eyes to block out the sun. The mother was so busy cuddling her child I could see she wasn't noticing anything so I said nothing. I didn't want to alarm her. Our bags were in the back and I was anxious to get out of the country as quickly as possible.

'Do you want to go to the airport?' the driver enquired.

'No,' I replied. The mother and daughter were travelling on their own passports and would be easy to stop if the alarm went up. We had to find a more discreet way out of Turkey. 'I want you to drive us to the border.'

'To Greece, or Bulgaria?' he enquired.

'I don't think so,' I said, thinking on my feet. 'That's the direction they would be expecting us to go in. I want you to take us east to Kurdistan.'

He let out a sharp whistle at the thought of such a long drive but didn't argue. The fare for the journey would give him enough money to live for several weeks. We settled down for a tedious trip along endless winding roads. It took hours and once we reached Kurdistan we paid him off and changed to another car. The scenery now became mostly desert as we headed south into Iraq and then round the edge of Syria and into Jordan, changing drivers at every border. I felt like some sort of nomad, constantly travelling, unable to tell one country from another whenever I woke from a fitful doze. The mother cuddled her child to her for most the trip, the two of them drifting in and out of sleep, not saying much, apparently content just to be in one another's company. I felt pretty confident that the Turkish authorities would never expect us to follow such a circuitous route. Even if they did they wouldn't have any jurisdiction in the other countries since we were travelling with legal papers.

Once again we were living in cars and surviving off the snacks we could get from roadside stalls and garages. Occasionally we stopped in a village if we saw there was a shower in the street or other washing facilities. The little girl was very good. I guess to her it was all a great adventure. Because she was with her mother she didn't seem to be frightened by the strangeness of the surroundings. I think perhaps it was a great adventure for me, too. I was beginning to get used to life on the road. It can become addictive, having nothing to think about and endless passing scenery to stare at with an empty mind. After a while I almost didn't want the trip to end. I didn't want to return to a world where I would have to face up to choices and decisions and responsibilities. I became very nervous at every police checkpoint, since they always seemed to have to make a great pantomime out of studying our papers, as if we looked suspicious to them. I resented their intrusion into our little private world, but in fact none of them held us up for more than a few minutes.

Several days later we arrived back in Britain, battered and weary but triumphant. Things wouldn't always go so well. I was nearing the end of my lucky streak.

That mother managed to keep her cool very well at the moment of reunion. People weren't always so able to keep their emotions under control. One of them, on a mission to Morocco, completely ignored my warnings and ran over and grabbed her child the moment we saw him. It was nearly a disaster. The child was out on a shopping trip with a bunch of women who, I guess, were his paternal relatives. The moment she saw him in amongst the other women, the mother lost all control of her emotions, shrieking the child's name and rushing through the crowds of shoppers, barging and pushing people out of the way and drawing attention to herself. Luckily the women who were supposed to be looking after the child were so startled by this hysterical woman stampeding in their direction that they hesitated before stopping her and she was able to grab her son's hand and haul him away with her, shouting instructions to him as she went.

There was nothing I could do except join her as she dived down a side road with him flying in her wake. We didn't even have a car ready for our getaway. I hitched up my skirts and ran after them. By the time I caught them up the other women had gathered their thoughts and were giving chase too, shouting to passers-by to stop us because we were kidnappers.

My heart was pounding so loudly and I was so out of breath I was afraid I was going to collapse. I could imagine them catching up with me and carting me off to the police station, and the picture of a bare Moroccan prison cell kept me going despite the stitch in my chest and my aching legs.

We dodged down side alleys and round buildings, tripping over cats and litter, inciting a pack of stray dogs to run at our heels, barking joyfully at the excitement of the chase. Fortunately for us the other women seemed to be even less fit than we were and after a few twists and turns we realised we'd lost them. We collapsed in some shade, hidden behind a wall, in order to get our breath back, shooing the barking dogs away, frightened they would give us away with their stupid, overexcited yelps. We'd managed to escape but it was very unfair on the child who was deeply shocked and frightened by it all. It would have been much better to have waited for a moment when he was alone and his mother could talk to him gently and calmly rather than grabbing, screaming and running.

Things often failed to go according to plan on rescues. On another trip to Egypt we didn't discover until we got there that the child in question was living in a flat and not going to school. In fact there was never a moment of the day when she wasn't with a grown-up from the family, usually with her hand firmly held. The grown-ups also seemed to jump into taxis as quickly as possible whenever they left the house with her, as if they were nervous about being on the street for a minute longer than they had to be. So the mother and I had to change the method of operation that we'd been planning to use. If she wasn't going to school, we couldn't take her from there.

'If we're going to get her we're actually going to have to snatch her from her grandmother,' I said. 'She's the one in the family who's least likely to be able to catch up with us.'

'But she'll make a hell of a noise and may attract the attention of other passers-by who'll probably want to help,' the mother pointed out.

'I know,' I said, thinking hard. 'So we have to be ready to make a bloody quick getaway, preferably in a car. We don't want to be trapped in the street by an angry mob.'

In Egypt people have a habit of sharing taxis. If a taxi already has a customer and someone else hails it, the driver will stop to see if the second person is going in the same direction as the first, so that they can share the cost. I was watching someone doing just that when the idea hit me.

'We need to be in the cab when the grandmother comes out,' I explained. 'We'll cruise past slowly and hope she hails it, as we've seen her do before.'

The next day we were back in the same position in our taxi, watching and waiting. A few hours after we arrived the grandmother came out with the child. Our driver, who was fully briefed on what we planned to do and seemed to be enjoying the adventure, drew out and travelled slowly along behind her.

'Slow down,' I said. 'She hasn't seen you.'

He slowed to a crawl but still the woman didn't look round. We came level with her and I could hear the mother in the front seat letting out a little whimper as her child's head came alongside her open window.

'We'll have to turn round up ahead somewhere and come back past her,' I said.

'Taxi!' The grandmother's voice was clearly audible in the car. She'd just spotted us. The driver slammed on the brakes, almost sending me into the front seat and the mother through the windscreen. He waited, allowing the old woman to come puffing up behind us.

The mother of the child had her face covered and didn't look round from the front as the grandmother opened the back door and told the driver where she wanted to go. He nodded his agreement and she pushed the child into the middle of the back seat, next to me, and then levered herself in afterwards. I hadn't realised when watching her walking just what a huge woman she was. She barely seemed to fit through the door. Once she'd planted herself on the seat and closed the door after her, the child was squashed between us so tightly I worried that she might not be able to breathe. The girl's sharp little elbows were digging into me painfully and I tried to manoeuvre her into a more comfortable position, but that made the old woman tut and glare at me, so I stopped. I didn't want her to spend too much time looking at my face in case she had to identify me later for the police.

I could almost feel the tension in the mother's neck as she

forced herself not to look round at her baby. My heart was thumping so loudly I was sure the old woman must be able to hear it. She appeared not to even notice there was anyone else in the car with her, issuing instructions to the driver on which roads to go down and telling him alternately to slow down or hurry up.

'Drop me here!' she instructed imperiously and there was then a long struggle as she fought to get back out of the car. Eventually, muttering and cursing under her breath, she was free and standing on the pavement, fumbling in her bag for the money for the fare. The child was just sliding across the seat to follow her grandmother out when I caught hold of her arm, saying her name as gently as I could, and at the same time shouting at the driver to go. He stamped on the accelerator and I leaned across the startled little girl and pulled the door shut. The grandmother dropped her bag and was about to bend to pick it up when she realised the car was going with her granddaughter in it. The mother was leaning over the back of the front seat with her scarf pulled back, talking to the girl as we sped away into the traffic. The girl was leaning forward to embrace her mother, who hung on to her, kissing the top of her head and crying. Horns were honking all around us, making our nerves jangle even more.

Looking back I could see the grandmother shouting and waving her arms in the air, shouting at passers-by to help her. By the time we'd turned the corner a small, puzzled-looking crowd was beginning to form around her. I guessed there would be a lot of people giving her advice on what to do.

'I think we should change cars,' I said to the mother. 'She may have got the number of this one.'

The driver nodded his understanding and drove us to an area where there were a lot of other drivers waiting for fares. They all seemed to know him and he fell into conversation with one of them while we waited in the car. I'd changed places with the mother so that she could curl up on the back seat and hug her daughter properly. The little girl was watching everything that was going on around her with wide, frightened eyes. We could see the drivers looking towards us and gesticulating. After a few minutes the other man came over and introduced himself, and we moved to his car.

'We need to get back to our room at the Marriott,' I explained. 'To fetch our things.'

A few minutes later he had us there and while I packed up our belongings the mother went downstairs and paid the bill. Her daughter was now standing happily beside her, already becoming bored with the grown-up world and looking around for something more interesting to do. I'm always surprised how quickly the children adapt from being scared to being content to be with their mothers, wherever they might be taking them. I very much doubt if any small child is as comfortable with their father in an unfamiliar situation as with their mother. I realise that is a generalisation and there are bound to be exceptions, some of whom I have met, but as a general rule I'm convinced of it.

'We can't go to the airport,' I said as we made our way back to the cab. 'They're bound to be watching there. That woman will have been screaming blue murder down at the police headquarters within five minutes. We'll go by boat.'

The mothers are usually so wrapped up in the process of bonding with their children in the first few hours after a snatch that they're willing to let me deal with all the details of how to get away. I'm happy with that situation. I'm nearly always more familiar with the country we're in and its transport systems than they are and I prefer to be able to concentrate on that and leave them to look after the child.

We caught a boat to Cyprus that evening and flew back to Heathrow the next day from Cyprus Airport, a place that I've grown very familiar with over the years. The boats in that part of the world are not the most comfortable form of travel. The seas are invariably choppy and there is always an odour of vomit in the air, left from a thousand previous rough trips. I take a cabin if I can. Even though they're horrible cramped little rooms, at least they give you privacy in which to feel ill. You can usually lie down and there's often a small hand basin so you can rinse yourself off. The food on the ships is always inedible in the dining rooms and the tea stewed. The other passengers always seem to be carrying too much luggage, particularly those flimsy, stripy bags, which look as if they've been made from old-fashioned deckchair material, and bundles of material held together with string. Wherever you turn you fall over these bulging piles of belongings, often finding people asleep among them. Sea voyages invariably end up becoming endurance tests.

For the first few hours of any journey I'm always aware that we're still in the territorial waters of the country we've just escaped from, and I live in fear of being discovered, having the ship stopped and helicopters sent out to bring us back. I've learned a technique of always looking busy when the ticket collectors and officials come round. It doesn't matter whether its playing with a Gameboy or cards, or searching in my handbag for the tickets, I always want to look harassed and disorganised, as any mother on an innocent trip would do. I always think that if I look too well organised I will attract suspicion. Shouting impatiently at the children is another good way of distracting attention away from your face and your papers.

Sometimes on missions I would meet an unexpected level of resistance from the fathers. On one occasion I even found myself in danger of being shot.

I first saw Kate Hamilton, a part-time dental nurse, on morning television as I was wandering around the house, clearing up after getting the children off to school. Her words made me stop whatever I was doing to listen. She was talking about how her two daughters, Rana, who was seven, and Hanan, who was eleven, had been snatched by their father, Ali, in breach of a court order. They'd been spirited away to Jordan. It was a familiar-sounding story but she told it with great passion and my heart went out to her. Ali had told her he was taking the girls for a day-trip to Legoland and Kate's suspicions weren't raised until the children were already well beyond her reach in Jordan. It doesn't matter how often I hear stories like this, they still leave me horror struck, and I can immediately imagine myself in the mother's shoes: left alone, with her family having vanished.

Jordan is one of the countries that hasn't signed up to the Hague Agreement, which was designed to ensure that children who have been wrongfully removed from Britain would be returned by law. As a result, Kate had been told by every government official she'd spoken to that there was nothing they could do to help her, so she'd turned to the media in the hope that the British public would come to her assistance if they just heard her heartbreaking story. She obviously had the sympathy of the audience she was talking to, as well as the presenter.

I liked the sound of her immediately. I would have found it impossible to ignore her and not offer to do whatever I could. It was as if she was talking directly to me from the screen, as if that was the whole reason for her appearing on the show.

As soon as the programme was over I rang the television studio and managed to get put through to her. I told her a bit about who I was and what I'd done in the past and I asked if there was anything I could do to help. She sounded deeply grateful just to have someone show an interest and we made a date to meet.

When I met her I liked Kate even more than when I'd seen her on the screen. She seemed very genuine and warm and I could see how much pain she was in. She showed me pictures of two pretty, dark-eyed girls.

'I was 21 when I met Ali, their father,' she explained, once we were settled down with cups of coffee. 'He was so good looking and charming. He ran a local cab firm. He seemed to be so kind, not like other boys I'd met, and so attentive, as if I was the most important person in the world to him. I already had a daughter, Kira, from a previous relationship and he was really good with her. It's hard to meet people when you have a child, especially men who'll be willing to take on other men's children, but he never saw it as a problem.

'I thought I'd found a man I could spend the rest of my life with, bringing up a family together. I became pregnant, which we were both very happy about. He looked after me as if I was the most precious thing in the world. But once Hanan was born he seemed to change. He became very possessive of me, always wanting to know what I was doing and where I was going, and losing his temper if he thought I wasn't doing exactly what he wanted. He was frightening when he was angry and I probably should have got out of the relationship at that stage, but I didn't have the courage to leave him. I kept telling myself things would get better, that I should just be patient.

'I got pregnant again and I thought another baby might make things better. But when Rana came along things got worse and he started to be unkind to Kira, because she wasn't his daughter, I suppose. Everything I did seemed to be wrong in his eyes.'

If only I'd known her as a friend during this time I would have been able to warn her that these are all the classic signs of a man who's likely to abduct his children, even at that early stage. I could have advised her to start taking precautions like hiding the children's passports and papers and never allowing him to be alone with them both at once. But in fact Ali wasn't yet planning to take the children away from their mother.

'He wanted us all to move back to Jordan,' she explained, 'and I thought that perhaps he was being like this just because he was homesick. I thought if we went back to his native country, perhaps he would go back to being the way he'd been when we first met. I can see now I was being naïve, but you'll try anything in a situation like that, and you can't see things objectively. I was so unhappy I would have tried anything to make things better.'

She agreed to go out to Jordan with him, which was a reasonable thing to do in the circumstances. She was right that once there, among his own people, he might have settled down again and allowed the nice side of his nature, which she had seen when she first met him, to come through. It does sometimes happen and if the woman is comfortable living in the husband's family everything is all right.

'It was much worse over there,' she said, taking a sip of hot coffee, allowing her memory to go back to what must have been a difficult time for her. 'Ali just became angrier and angrier with us over every little thing. It was as if he hated Kira and me. The whole family treated Kira badly, just because she wasn't their blood. It was terrible. I desperately wanted to protect her but I couldn't be with her every second and they would be horrible to her even if I was there. I realised I'd done the wrong thing by taking her out there but I didn't know what to do to put things right. If I'd felt helpless to leave him in England, it seemed even harder in a strange country where I didn't know the language or the customs or anything. I felt completely trapped.

'My mum came out to visit and she could see how bad things were between us. She told me that I shouldn't put up with it, that I shouldn't be making Kira go through it. She gave me the courage I needed and I decided to leave. But I didn't have any money. "Don't worry," she told me before she left, "I'll find a way of getting some money to you." She started sending out presents for the girls from England, things like dolls, and she would roll up £50 notes inside them. She did brilliantly and I managed to keep the money hidden until I had enough. I knew I'd have to run away in secret. Ali would never have agreed to the girls going with me. Eventually, after a few months, I had enough money and I managed to get all four of us on a flight to Britain.

'Once I got here I was really scared that he'd come after us. I'd met some of his friends out in Jordan and they seemed like ruthless men to me. As soon as I landed I went into hiding. I even changed my name by deed poll to try to make it harder for him to find us. It was an awful thing to have to do, but it was better than the alternatives. I thought that we would be able to start our lives again and that after a few years, when he knew the girls were grown up, he would give up looking for us.'

Kate had underestimated Ali's determination. It only took him six months to find them and turn up on their doorstep. I could just imagine how she must have felt, opening the front door and seeing him standing there. But things seemed to have changed. It was as if she'd jolted him into a realisation that he'd been acting badly and he was determined to make amends.

'He was back to being his charming old self again,' she explained. 'The man I'd fallen in love with all those years ago, and he won my confidence back. Not immediately, but bit by bit, lulling me into a false sense of security. I gradually allowed him to see more and more of the girls, although I never trusted him completely. I made sure I had a court ruling, which forbade him from taking them out of the country.'

Ali must have been a very patient man because he worked on Kate for three years before he made his move, defying the court ruling and flying the children back to Jordan after telling Kate he was taking them to Legoland for the day.

'That was nine months ago,' she said. 'And I haven't seen or heard a word from them since.'

I knew I had to help. I couldn't imagine how desperate I would be feeling after nine months of not knowing where my children were.

'I want them back,' Kate said eventually. 'Please help me.'

'Of course I'll help,' I said. 'But we may not be able to get them back that easily. Taking two children is much harder than one, and it sounds like your husband will be guarding them carefully. He must know that you're trying to reach them through the media.'

'If I could just see them,' she said, 'to know they're all right and to let them know that I haven't forgotten them and that I'm looking for them.'

I promised that I'd do whatever I could to help. We met several times over the next few months and prepared our plans. Kate had already been to the Foreign Office to try to get help but, like so many others before her, had realised that, however many sympathetic noises they might make, there was nothing the civil service or government could do for her. She was going to have to try to get to the girls herself. The problem with official government departments and large organisations is that they have to abide by the letter of the law and they have to be careful not to upset diplomatic relations between countries. That often means that their hands are tied and there's nothing they can do to help an individual, or whatever they can do will take years, by which time the children have grown up and the damage has been done. It's like going to a hospital with a broken neck and being told that there are procedures which have to be gone through and you are unlikely to get treated for a few years. When you lose your small children it's an emergency and every day counts. Kate needed immediate help from someone who knew their way around the Middle East and I was more than happy to fulfil that role in any way I could. Every passing day without her children was making her feel worse; the panic that she might never see them again was mounting, along with the fear that the girls would be adults by the time they were reunited with her. I couldn't possibly have resisted her pleas for help.

She was engaged to a guy called Steve, and the three of us set off for Jordan together. We didn't know exactly where the kids would be, but we were determined to keep looking until we found them. Once we'd located them we'd work out a strategy for getting to see them or, possibly, bringing them back to Britain. For the first few days we hired a local driver who took us around trying to track down the one address that Kate had for Ali's parents' home. Although she'd been there in the past she'd never taken much notice of how to get there, just being a passenger while other people drove. She was sure she would recognise it once we saw it.

There was a strong possibility that the children would be there. If a man from that part of the world is alone with children, and not rich enough to hire maids and chauffeurs, it's always likely that he will take them back to his mother. The parents are usually very happy to have their sons and grandchildren back home. It's all part of the family culture, which is so prevalent in the area and which is the rock upon which their society is founded. It was just these sorts of powerful family ties that had first attracted me to the Muslim religion and way of life. When it works well and the daughter-in-law is part of the family, it's the best set-up imaginable, but when she's excluded by her husband, for whatever reason, the rest of the clan tends to unite forces against her.

At the end of the second day we found the house. It was part of small hamlet, a fair way from the nearest town and quite exposed. There was nowhere close by where a car could stand for any length of time without attracting attention, especially if it contained two women and two men, just sitting there, watching. So we drove to the other side of the valley and found a place where we could see the house but where we would be hidden from sight amongst the rocks. It was hot and dry and one of us had to stay awake at all times in case someone came in or out and we missed them. Everything was still and silent on both sides of the valley, the houses shuttered up against the blazing sun. Apart from the occasional lizard flickering across the rocks, nothing moved around us. It was as if the whole world was holding its breath to see what would happen next. At least when we were working in towns and cities there were other distractions to take our minds off the boredom of the job, and one or other of us could leave the car from time to time to bring back refreshments or even just go for a walk and look at the street life. Here there was nowhere to go and nothing to watch apart from the featureless view. It wasn't the sort of terrain for taking a pleasant stroll.

'This is ridiculous,' I said after several hours of tedium. 'For all we know, we're watching an empty house. We need to at least find out if there's anyone in there.'

'How are we going to do that without arousing their suspicions?' Kate asked.

'They have no reason to be on their guard out here,' I said. 'They'd never imagine you'd go to the trouble of finding them in such a desolate area. As long as they don't spot you we should be all right. I'll go over with the driver and ask for some water. I'll let him do the talking in case my accent gives me away.'

We discussed the plan for a while and eventually, realising that we might be sitting behind those rocks for weeks with no result, Kate agreed. The driver and I set off. Nothing and no one stirred as we arrived among the houses. There didn't even seem to be any dogs or cats. It was like a ghost town. We went to the house Kate had pointed out to us and knocked on the door. It remained resolutely shut and the windows stayed tightly shuttered. I put my ear to the wood to see if I could hear voices or the shuffling of people getting out of sight. There was no sound at all.

'There might be another door,' the driver suggested and I nodded my agreement. I tugged my scarf forward a little to shade my face from the ferocity of the sun's rays. We went gingerly round the back to see if there was a back entrance, but there was nothing. It looked as if the house had been closed up for several days at least.

'There's no one there,' I said, when we got back to the car. 'Are there any other addresses we could follow up?'

'Ali did have a brother who lived in Amman,' Kate said. 'I have an old address for a flat, but I have no idea if he's still there. I never had much to do with him. He seemed like a nasty piece of work to me quite dangerous.'

'It's got to be worth a try,' I said. 'Anything is better than sitting here for the next few days. We can always come back here later.'

We drove back to Amman city and started searching the streets for the address that Kate had. The names were confusing and it took the best part of another day before we found the place we wanted. It was a large block of flats, which didn't look old but was already showing signs of wear and tear. There was a threatening atmosphere about the place. It didn't look like strangers would be welcome here. If the heat in the countryside had been bad, the city was even worse. The streets were airless and the atmosphere in the car was beginning to become fetid and unpleasant. We found a place where we could park and see the entrance of the flat, without being too noticeable, and settled down once more to watching and waiting. Nothing happened.

'I'm going to nose around a bit,' I said after a couple of hours, when I thought I was about to go mad with the heat and the waiting. 'I'll ask the neighbours some questions; check we're on the right track. There's no point us sitting here for days on end if they aren't here.'

'Be careful,' Kate cautioned. 'These aren't nice people.'

I nodded my understanding of her warning, but I was determined to get things moving. It seemed quite likely the children weren't here either, in which case we could move on and get some air into the car, and perhaps even find beds for the night in air-conditioned rooms.

I climbed out of the car, adjusted my headscarf and strolled across the road as casually as I could. I wandered around the block, nodding and exchanging greetings with women sitting at their windows or dozing in the shade. They seemed wary but not openly hostile to a stranger. When I found a group who seemed particularly friendly I paused and complained about the heat. They agreed and offered me a seat in the shade with them. We chatted about the neighbourhood for a while and I made up a story about how I was married to a Jordanian and was returning to Amman. I said I was looking for somewhere to live where there would be English-speaking children for mine to play with. They brought me a glass of water and some children ran past. I asked if there were a lot of children in the block and eventually, after going round the houses a few times, I managed to bring the conversation to the two girls.

'Yes,' one of the women, an old crone with a giant mole on her lip and big, gappy teeth, told me, 'I know the girls you mean. They've been living in that flat. They're lovely girls but they don't go out much.'

We chatted on for a while and then I thanked them for the water, bade them goodbye and ambled back round the corner to the car.

'They're in there,' I said, sinking back into my seat.

'Oh,' Kate sounded as if she might cry, with a mixture of relief and shock at finally having found her babies. Her eyes had watered up, but she put a brave face on it. 'What do we do now? Are they all right?'

'The women say they don't come out often, so there's not much chance we'll be able to get to them while they're playing in the street. Ali must be keeping them under close watch.'

I thought for a moment.

'Did you tell me your sister-in-law worked as a teacher in the local international school?'

'Yes.' Kate nodded. 'If they're going to school that's where Ali would send them.'

'Let's go and ask around there then,' I said. 'If they are going there then we may be able to take them from there, or on the way from the house in the morning.'

Kate gave the driver instructions and we drove closer. I

didn't want to stay in one place for too long anyway, in case we started to arouse suspicion. We re-parked in some shade across the street from the school.

'You'd better cover your face up,' I said. 'In case we bump into your sister-in-law or the girls.'

'OK.' Kate pulled on her veil and I adjusted my scarf, leaving my face bare as I planned to do the talking. We walked in and I asked to see the headmistress.

'I'm from a diplomatic family and we are moving back to Amman. I'm looking for a school for my two girls,' I explained.

She was very friendly and more than happy to show us around the premises even though we hadn't made an appointment. It was a nice school, and all the children smiled as they passed us.

'A friend of mine teaches here,' I said, naming Ali's sister. 'She recommended that we come to see you.'

'Ah yes,' the headmistress smiled. 'I'm afraid she's left us now.' We strolled from classroom to classroom and the headmistress explained what each group of children were doing. There was no sign of Rana or Hanan in any of the classes for their age group.

After a reasonable amount of time, I thanked her sincerely for being so helpful, promised to come back with my children so they could see what a nice place it was for themselves and we left.

'It doesn't look like they're enrolled in any school around here,' I said once we were back in the car. 'Because if they were, that would be the one.'

'You mean they're locked up inside some poky little flat all day with nothing to do and nowhere to go?' Kate fumed. 'And he isn't even bothering to get them an education!'

'Looks like it,' I agreed. 'Unless this is just a temporary hideout and he plans to take them somewhere else soon and enrol them for their education there. If that's the case then we need to act fast before they get moved on and we lose them forever.'

'How are we going to get to them if they never come out of the flat?' Steve wanted to know. 'We can hardly break the doors down and grab them.'

'I don't know,' I admitted. 'I don't think we have any option but to show our faces and ask if Kate can just see the kids and talk to them. At least if we can establish some sort of communication there's a hope that we'll be able to get a reasonable arrangement at a later date.'

'But I want them back,' Kate said tearfully.

'I know,' I said, squeezing her hand, 'but seeing them would be better than nothing, wouldn't it?'

'Yes.' She nodded, 'I suppose so. I've certainly had enough of sitting around in this car. Any positive action would be better than nothing.'

I could see that her usual spirit was returning. 'OK,' I said. 'Let's go and knock on the door. I don't see that we have anything to lose.'

'I'm coming too,' Steve said. 'I'm not having you two going in there on your own.'

'OK,' I agreed. I could see it would make sense to have a

man along, since we had no idea what was waiting for us behind those shutters.

We made our way to the door of the flat and knocked. After a few moments a woman's voice came from the other side, asking what we wanted. That was a good sign. A woman might well have sympathy for a mother who'd been separated from her children; we might be able to get inside and at least see the children before Ali returned and interfered.

'It's Kate, the children's mother,' I called back in Arabic. 'She's come to visit Rana and Hanan.'

'Go away!' the woman shouted. Her voice sounded frightened but I couldn't tell if she was frightened for us or for herself. 'Go away now!'

'We don't want to cause any trouble,' I assured her. 'Kate just wants to visit the girls.'

'You can't come in here,' she shouted back. 'Go now or I'll call the police.'

'Mummy, Mummy!' a small girl's voice rang out, but was quickly muffled, as if someone had put a hand over her mouth.

'Rana?' Kate screamed. 'Rana, is that you?'

She started to beat her fists on the door that was separating her from her children. It was agonising to see the look on her face and to hear her calling out to her daughter, knowing someone inside was holding her against her will. It was obvious that the woman was never going to let us in and it seemed likely there were other people inside the flat with her. Steve and I persuaded Kate to come away with us for a while.

'We'll come back in a bit,' I promised. 'Let's just let things calm down and give her time to think the situation through.'

Kate nodded despondently. She could see the sense of what I was saying but the thought of moving even one step further away from her babies was obviously torture. I guess she was frightened they might have been taken away again by the time we came back.

None of us wanted to go back to the car so we walked to a café and found a shaded table. Several pairs of eyes followed us as we sat down. No doubt our raised voices had carried a long way in the hot afternoon air. People would be on their guard against us now. We were outsiders, causing a disturbance in their area. We needed to tread carefully. We ordered some drinks and spent an hour going over and over the options that lay before us, even though there were hardly any to choose from. It was obvious that Kate wasn't going to go anywhere without having another go at getting to her girls. I'm sure I would have felt the same in her position. Would any mother be able to walk away from her children if she knew where they were? Could any mother actually hear their voices and not go back to try to reach them? I don't think so.

'OK,' I said eventually, 'I agree we have to have another try while we're sure they're still there. But let's go and get the car so we can park closer and make a quick getaway if we need to. If Ali or his brother are back they'll be expecting us and from what you've told us it's possible they might be violent.'

The others agreed and we walked back to where our driver was patiently waiting. We drove round the corner to the front of the block.

'Oh shit!' I exclaimed.

Whoever had been inside the flat had obviously called for reinforcements the moment we'd gone away. The place had taken on the appearance of a domestic fortress. There were now four unpleasant-looking men standing outside the flat, obviously on guard and looking for us. One of them was checking his gun and the others looked as if they were armed as well. Why else would they have been wearing jackets in that heat? It seemed that Ali was willing to take the battle to a violent level in order to keep his girls away from their mother.

'Look, it's Rana!' Kate shouted, pointing to a window where a little hand was frantically waving at us. She waved back and the action alerted one of the men to the presence of our car. He glanced up at the window to see what Kate was waving at, just as someone inside pulled Rana back out of sight. The guard shouted to his companions and they all turned to look at the car.

'Quick!' I shouted to the driver. 'Get out of here!'

He could see the danger as clearly as we could. He stamped on the accelerator and we screeched away as the four men ran to the road and pulled open the doors of a blue saloon car, which was parked in front of the flats. The men scrambled in and we heard the roar of an engine being revved, followed by another screech of tyres. Our driver had a head start, but their car was obviously more powerful. We hurtled through the streets of Amman, our tyres screaming in protest as we tore round corners, sending pedestrians jumping to the sides. I could smell the powerful scent of burning rubber in the air. It was terrifying, but not as terrifying as the thought of what those four men would do if they caught up with us.

Our driver was good, but he was obviously panicking. He was driving much too fast and didn't seem to have full control of the car. Once or twice we mounted the pavements or grazed along low walls, but he kept going. On one corner he knocked off his wing mirror with a bang as loud and shocking as a gunshot. We all let out shouts of fear, then laughed nervously when we realised what it was. Every time I turned round the blue car was still there and at times I could even see the angry, determined faces of the men in the front seats, just a few feet away from us.

After what seemed like an age, hanging on to the straps and being tossed around inside the car, our heads banging on the roof and our shoulders against the sides, we were out of the built-up area and driving at full speed along the edge of a ravine. The car was swerving from side to side and a cloud of dust was rising up behind us. We all let out involuntary screams as the wheels banged against the edge and we saw the ravine opening up below us. If we came off the road here we'd be goners, but if the men behind caught up with us we might be just as dead. Now that we were out of town there were fewer people and there might be no one to witness our execution if it happened at the side of a deserted road. All these thoughts and more were going through my head as we bumped and crashed through potholes and zigzagged from side to side.

The chase went on for a terrible hour and a half. Every muscle in my body was aching from the effort of holding on and every joint felt bruised and battered. I began to worry that we might run out of petrol and be forced to stop and fight for our lives. I leaned across to look at the gauge and saw that it was hovering down at a quarter full. I turned round to see how close our pursuers were.

'They're stopping!' I shouted, as the dust cloud cleared to show the empty road behind us. I hardly dared to believe what I was seeing.

'Maybe they've run out of petrol first,' Steve suggested.

'Keep going for a while,' I told the driver, 'and then try to find another way back to Amman.'

Our belongings were at the hotel we'd checked into on first arriving in the country. I was anxious to retrieve them and to move to another hotel, one that would be less conspicuous. When we got back to the hotel I made the driver wait in the road outside for a while before we got out, to see if the blue saloon was anywhere around. I didn't want to get up to the rooms and find them waiting for us. When I was reasonably confident that the coast was clear we made our way upstairs, hurriedly collected our things and went back downstairs to pay the bill. I was glancing over my shoulder the whole time, certain that it wouldn't be long before they started checking the big hotels to find where we were staying.

Once the bill had been paid our driver took us to a small backstreet hotel that he knew of. It wasn't as comfortable as the one we'd just left, but it felt safer and when we got to our rooms we rested for a while, preparing ourselves for the next move.

I felt we were out of our depth and thought we needed more local help. I rang the friend who lived in Amman and had helped me out on previous missions. I explained the situation in brief and asked for advice. He came straight over to the hotel to see us. We explained what had happened in more detail and described where the flat was.

'Could you go back and just see if there are still men around, or whether it would be safe for us to try again?' I asked, my courage beginning to return.

'Sure,' he said.

An hour later he was back at the hotel. 'You won't get near the place,' he told us. 'There's an armed guard on the roof and another in front of the flat.'

None of us intended to risk going back as long as they were there, but what else could we do? If the girls never came out, and we couldn't get in, it was stalemate. We sat around in my room for hours going over and over our options. A knock on the door made us all jump. Had they managed to track us down already?

'Who is it?' I called out in Arabic.

'We're from the British Consul,' came the reply in English.

'Oh God,' I said to the others.

'How do we know it isn't them?' Steve asked.

I went to the peephole in the door. There were three of them and they looked British. I opened the door and their spokesman explained why they were there.

'The Special Police want to talk to you. They're waiting downstairs in the lobby. We persuaded them to let us come up and find you rather than charging into the room themselves.'

Kate and I exchanged looks. I wasn't sure if this was good news or bad.

'Would you come down and talk to them?' he asked.

I didn't think I had any choice but to believe them.

'We'll have to go down,' I told the others. 'These people don't just go away if you ignore them.'

We left the room and followed the three officials downstairs to the hotel lobby where the local Special Police officers were waiting, looking more than a little uncomfortable at their assignment. It appeared that word of what we were up to had spread through Amman rather faster than I'd expected. It seemed Ali was willing to do everything possible to keep the girls away from their mother, even if it meant involving the authorities and sending them to track us down. The officers wanted to know what we were doing in Jordan. There didn't seem much point lying now. I explained that Kate's girls had been taken away from her nearly a year before and she wanted to see them. The police listened to us with barely disguised impatience and then advised us to leave on the next available flight. We were obviously a considerable inconvenience and they didn't want to spend any longer on the case than they had to. If we just disappeared back to Britain they could pretend we'd never been there.

'I'm not just going to abandon my children,' Kate said, horrified at the thought.

'Then we'll have no option but to arrest you,' the police spokesman sighed. 'We cannot risk another incident like today.'

'Arrested?' Kate looked shocked. It probably hadn't occurred to her that this could happen. 'All I want to do is see my children. What crime have I committed?'

'You'll have to do what they say, Kate,' I counselled. 'You don't want to get put into a prison out here. You could be in there for months before the case even came to court. And what good would that do Rana and Hanan anyway? It would just frighten them even more to think of their mummy locked up in a cell.'

She started crying again and I could see the police were uncomfortable, not knowing how to handle the situation. The men from the British Consul looked equally ill at ease. They were obviously powerless, just there to witness proceedings in case anything went badly wrong.

'OK,' I told them quietly, 'we'll go. Give us time to pack.'

I took Kate up to her room and made sure Steve was looking after her. I've never seen a woman look so downhearted. The thought of leaving the country without even having hugged her girls and told them how much she loved them was breaking her heart. She must have been imagining what they would be feeling and thinking after hearing her voice outside their front door and seeing her pass by the window. I was determined to have one more try at arranging a meeting, but I didn't say anything to Kate or Steve, not wanting to raise their hopes again in case I failed. Once I'd settled them in their room I left the hotel and went down to the headquarters of the Special Police on my own.

As soon as I was inside I let go of all my restraint. I made as much fuss as I could, my voice echoing round the building, until I was taken to the most senior officer, just to shut me up. Once I was in his office I immediately calmed down and explained how important it was for Kate to see the girls before she left. I promised that if they would just allow us one meeting I would guarantee to take her back to England and we wouldn't cause any more trouble in the streets of Amman. I explained that the situation could only be resolved by the two sides talking to each other and that we had no intention of snatching the children or hurting them in any way. I said we all respected Ali and thought he was a fine father, but I also thought Kate was a fine mother and should be treated fairly.

I think there are very few people who could turn down such a heartfelt plea if it's put to them the right way. Everyone has a mother and I'm sure this man had a wife and children as well. He must have been able to put himself in our position.

'Very well,' he said eventually, 'but the meeting must be here, not at the flat or the hotel. We must be able to keep control of the situation.'

'Will you arrange for the girls to be brought here?' I asked.

'I will arrange that, yes,' he said. 'But you must promise me that the mother will not cause any trouble. She must come on her own.'

I promised and rushed back to the hotel as fast as I could to break the good news. Kate almost squeezed me to death in her excitement and a few minutes later we were tearing through the suitcases to find the presents friends and relatives had sent for the girls and collecting up the letters which we'd brought with us from their school friends and the favourite toys that they'd left behind when they were abducted and that Kate knew they'd be missing. Steve and I waited at the hotel as Kate set off to see her girls. There must have been a hundred thoughts going through her mind. What would they look like after so long? How would they have changed? What would they feel towards her? How would they behave at the meeting? Steve and I had no idea what was happening until later.

When she got to the police station Kate was told that there were strict rules governing the meeting. 'Only you can go in,' the police told her. 'No one else. And only for an hour.'

She thought about protesting at this restriction but realised it was the best offer they were likely to make and that it wouldn't have taken much for them to cancel the whole meeting and drive us straight to the airport. As Steve and I sat in the hotel wondering what was happening, picturing just how hard it must be for her, Kate was led away to a room where the girls were waiting for her. It did occur to me that Steve's presence in the country may have inflamed the situation. The fathers of children in broken marriages nearly always feel very resentful and jealous of any new partners the women might have. It's often the arrival of a stepfather in the picture, however nice a man he might be, which drives the natural father to think of abducting his children in the first place. Knowing that Kate was trying to get the children back, Ali might have felt doubly threatened by the idea of his children being taken away from him by another man.

Exactly an hour later, Kate came out of the room and

returned to the hotel. When she arrived in the room her face was streaked with tears and she was trembling uncontrollably. She fell into Steve's arms, crying her heart out.

'It was awful,' she sobbed. 'They clung to me the whole time. They had to prise Rana off me at the end like a little leech. Her fingers were clinging on so tightly I thought my sleeves were going to be ripped off. All I could think to do was hug them and kiss them and tell them how much I loved them. Hanan told me not to worry because she was looking after Rana for me. They looked so pale from being cooped up in that flat. They were always playing outside when they were in England. It's just not fair.'

I could imagine how devastated she felt. If I'd only seen my children for an hour in nine months and I was now going to have to board a plane and travel 2,000 miles away from them, knowing that they weren't happy where they were, I'd have been inconsolable as well. In fact I don't know if I would have been strong enough to do it, but the deal had been struck and we had promised to leave Jordan after the meeting, so that was what we were going to have to do. I guess it was better for Kate than having to leave without seeing them at all, but not much.

We had a few hours to kill before we had to leave for the airport. We sat in my room, going over and over what had happened, all feeling deeply miserable. Kate was really grateful to me for arranging the meeting but it was so little compared to what we'd hoped to achieve when we first set out from England. If you're hoping to get your children back for good and only get an hour with them the pain must be unbearable. I was so full of admiration for her at being able to keep going at all, and glad she had Steve there to support her.

The phone in the room rang and when I picked it up a man's voice spoke.

'You're going to be killed,' he hissed.

The others didn't hear the message but could see I was shaken. I slammed the phone down as if it had stung me, and they made me tell them what had happened. There were several more calls, in which the same threat was made, before it was time to leave. Each time the phone rang I thought about not answering it, but was afraid we might miss some important last-minute development.

Receiving a death threat is the most alarming experience. Although you tell yourself that it's only words and there is a big gap between someone threatening to do something and actually doing it, the very fact that anyone feels so strongly about you that they're even willing to utter the words is totally unnerving. How could anyone think that someone who was just doing the best they could to solve a difficult situation deserved to be killed? I was more shocked and shaken than I would have expected, particularly as I knew that the issuers of the threats had access to guns and were willing to drive someone off the road in a high-speed car chase. If I felt vulnerable in the hotel room, aware that they knew exactly where we were, it was even worse stepping out into the street. I found myself searching the rooftops for signs of a sniper's rifle as we made our way quickly to the waiting taxi, behaving like some presidential bodyguard.

As the taxi headed through the streets towards the airport my eyes were continually darting from side to side, expecting at any moment to see a man coming towards us with a gun, or a car appearing beside us and trying to run us off the road in true action-movie style. Every passer-by looked suspicious and my heart was thumping so hard it was making me feel faint. I didn't say anything to the others and I could see that Kate was too overcome by her own private grief to worry about anything outside the car. When you're feeling as unhappy as she must have been at that moment the idea of death doesn't seem so frightening. By the time we arrived at the airport my legs felt weak and I could hardly walk. The others looked equally ashen and miserable as we went through the motions of checking in and moving our luggage through the system.

All three of us were crying on the plane as it took off. I was crying because I believed I'd let them down and Steve was upset to see Kate suffering. I think I might also have been crying with relief at being safely off the ground and out of the country. It was a terrible experience.

Once she was back in England Kate frequently tried to ring the girls, but whichever adult answered the phone would always hang up as soon as they realised who it was. It seems there can be no end to her agony until the girls are old enough to come looking for their mother themselves. It must have felt to her as if a large part of herself had died on that trip; all the high hopes that we had set out with snuffed out.

We had done our best to restore her children to her and we'd been beaten. It was the most saddening and disillusioning of experiences. I'd always liked to think that you can achieve anything if you really set your mind to it, but I could see that in Kate's case we'd come up against a brick wall. We'd taken on a foe too powerful. Because of his willingness to resort to violence and because of the labyrinthine international laws and diplomatic protocols which surround every tug of love, we could do nothing to defeat him. The injustice of it made me want to scream. How could anyone limit the contact a woman has with her children to one hour? One hour a day would be a scandal, but one hour in total? It defied belief.

CHAPTER NINE

My Cover Blown

THROUGHOUT ALL THESE adventures I'd managed to remain pretty anonymous as far as the general public was concerned. Although the people I'd worked with obviously got to know my name and often met my family, or even stayed with us, most outsiders never knew me as anything more than 'Dee', and often didn't even have a phone number for me. I was always anxious to protect my family in case someone who felt I'd wronged them came after my children. I knew that what I was doing was controversial and I believed that there might be people who would disagree with me so strongly they would try to harm us. The death threats I'd received during those last few hours in Jordan made me doubly aware that I didn't want to be receiving those sorts of calls at home. My children often answered the phone, particularly Marlon, and I didn't want them to be exposed to the sort of fear I'd experienced that day in Amman. There are enough unavoidable things in the world today to frighten them without introducing new ones. Marlon is now worryingly aware of the news and, when Tony Blair announced that Saddam Hussein had the capability of striking Cyprus with missiles, he became extremely anxious for the safety of his father and grandparents, believing that they were in imminent danger. Although I reassured him that just because he had the capability Saddam wouldn't necessarily make a strike, I know that I did not put his mind completely at rest.

All parents try their hardest to protect their children from the realities that surround us, but it's impossible to shelter them from all danger.

Despite my attempts at remaining anonymous, people who wanted to make contact with me always seemed to find a way to get word to me and I would ring them back on my mobile when their stories reached me. I knew we could never be completely safe, but at least I knew I'd made every effort to protect my family. It was also important that my real name stayed as much of a secret as possible so that I could pass over international borders without my passport attracting attention. If I became too well known for snatching children, or my face was plastered over the media, I would never be able to get into any country in the Middle East or North Africa again without false papers, which would increase the risks of being sent to prison if I was caught. The more recognisable I was the greater the likelihood I would be spotted.

Inevitably, the story of what I'd been doing had started to

filter through to the media. Journalists from magazines and researchers from television programmes were putting out the word that they wanted to talk to me. That put me in a quandary. On the one hand I didn't want my name or face to be published or broadcast for anyone to see, but at the same time I did want to publicise what I had been doing. I thought it would be helpful to the many thousands of women each year whose children are snatched and don't believe they can do anything about getting them back to know there are others in the same predicament. I wanted to show them that they should not bother with going to the law. If they just got out there and fought for their rights they'd stand a much better chance of seeing their children again. I also wanted women who were in mixed partnerships to be aware of the dangers, to be able to look out for the signs that the fathers of their children might be planning to take them away. I was beginning to think that getting the message out was more important than guarding my own privacy and anonymity.

Although I continued to use the name Dee, I started to agree to appear on television chat shows and current affairs programmes, and to talk to journalists when they managed to make contact with me. It was like dipping my toe into a swimming pool and I was surprised to find the water quite warm. I didn't receive any unpleasant feedback from the public. It seemed that just about everyone felt that what I was doing was right, even if I sometimes made mistakes and my methods were a little unorthodox. I still wanted to keep my anonymity as much as possible, but in 2002 all hope of that disappeared when I became part of a worldwide front-page story and nearly lost my own freedom.

I met Sarra Fotheringham through the *Trisha Show* a daytime television chat show that I'd appeared on. That sort of introduction was starting to happen quite often. Someone would see me on television or read about me in a magazine or newspaper and decide that I might be able to help them. The show's production team emailed me, saying there was a woman who was trying to get in touch with me and passed on her details. I would always respond to anyone who asked to talk to me, because they must be in a great deal of pain if they're coming to me for help. I couldn't possibly ignore their requests to be heard, even if I end up not being able to do anything to help. Sometimes, when you're in a situation like the ones these women find themselves in, just coming across someone who's willing to listen and be sympathetic is a help. It doesn't hurt me to spend a few hours drinking coffee and providing a sympathetic ear to someone who has lost the thing they care about most.

I rang the number the production team had given me and introduced myself to Sarra. Although I didn't recognise the name immediately, when she told me she'd been an air hostess and had had a child with a man from Dubai, I was pretty sure that I remembered hearing about her case on *Tonight With Trevor McDonald*, the late-night news review programme which I had also appeared on myself later on.

Over the phone she told me she lived in Camberley, a genteel Surrey town outside London, and we arranged to meet for coffee at my usual venue, Café Rouge on the first floor of Whiteleys, the scene of so many of my emotional first meetings with bereft mothers. When I saw her approaching the café I could tell she was a bit different from most of the women I'd been helping. She didn't look as crushed by life as many of them did. She had a jaunty air of self-confidence about her and was immaculately groomed. There was no question of her shrouding herself in headscarves and shapeless brown clothes.

She joined me, ordered a coffee and we started to talk. I didn't know if she was nervous about the meeting or whether she was always like that, but she struck me as a bit affected. It seemed as if she was trying to convince the world, and perhaps herself, that she was a bit more posh than she actually was. She was wearing jeans and cowboy boots in a sort of imitation Sloane style, which seemed just a little bit too perfect to be genuine. But I wasn't going to turn someone down just because they talked with a plum in their mouth and spent time on their grooming. She was still a mother who'd lost a child and needed my help. She told me she had been the woman I'd seen on *Tonight With Trevor McDonald* a few weeks before. I was impressed by the amount of media coverage she had succeeded in getting. If she'd managed to convince this many hard-bitten journalists and television producers of the worthiness of her cause, then I was more than willing to listen to what she had to say.

'I'm at my wits' end,' she told me, in her crystal clear diction.

'I've already been to see three organisations that claim to rescue children, one in England, one in South America and one in the Netherlands, but they quoted me £40,000, with no guarantees of success. I don't have that sort of money.'

I tutted sympathetically. I knew all about these sorts of mercenaries who make big promises, charge big fees and then don't always come up with the goods. Several of them had approached me and suggested I should work for them. I told them I preferred to remain independent. They were mostly ex-SAS soldiers, or at least claimed to be, the sort of people who were used to killing people to get what they wanted. One of them had assured me that he was an ex-FBI agent, a martial arts expert, a firearms expert, an authority on terrorism and a helicopter pilot, among other things. Since I can't even drive a car I wondered how I'd managed to achieve as many rescues as I had, particularly as they all insisted that they needed to charge huge fees in order to obtain the necessary expertise and access for each job. I hadn't felt comfortable about having anything to do with any of them, so I could quite understand why Sarra had decided not to avail herself of any of their services.

'You won't have to pay me anything beyond covering my expenses,' I assured her. 'I'm not in this to earn a living.'

She told me the story of how her son, 11-year-old Tariq, had been taken from her on a trip to Dubai to see his father.

'I've been fighting for two years to get him back,' she explained. 'One custody battle after another. It's like a nightmare. The father is Rashid Al-Habtoor. The Al-Habtoors are one of the wealthiest families in Dubai, very close to the ruling family. Whenever I do see him, or get an email from him, TT – that's what I call my son – tells me he doesn't want to be there. That he wants to be back with me.

'He was born and brought up over here as an English child, as part of an English family. It isn't natural for him to be 2,000 miles away over there, separated from his mother and his adopted father, who loves him, and his brothers and sister. Out there he's raised by servants and only sees his father for a couple of hours a week. It's not natural.

'The Al-Habtoors don't love him. They just want him because he's Rashid's eldest son. They want to keep him with them and groom him up to take over one of their businesses. But he's still just a little boy.'

Her big, immaculately made-up eyes were glistening with tears as she talked, nineteen to the dozen, and my heart went out to her. Tariq, she explained, had been the result of a romantic fling with this Rashid Al-Habtoor and her getting pregnant had caused the relationship to end in bitterness.

'We met through horse riding,' she told me. 'I was working as a stewardess for Emirates Airlines and on one stop-over I went to a stables near the Metropolitan Hotel, which was where Rashid kept his polo ponies. Rashid's father owned the stables and the hotel as well. I was only 23 years old. We got talking and he asked me out to dinner. He'd just come back from America and was very Western in his ways. He didn't talk about his family or his religion. He was very charming, very educated, very amusing. I could tell he was wealthy, but I had no idea how wealthy. What I also didn't know was that his family had already arranged for him to marry another girl.'

I remembered my own brush with a wealthy Arab family and the way in which they had managed to coax their son away from me and into an arranged marriage with a cousin. This sounded like an identical scenario so I had no reason to disbelieve her. Everything Sarra was saying had the ring of truth from my own experience. She went on to tell me she'd come back to England to have the baby when Rashid made it clear that he didn't want anything to do with it, accusing her of deliberately getting pregnant in order to entrap him, and claiming that the baby wasn't his anyway.

When Tariq was born I sent a note to Rashid, informing him he had a son. Later I discovered he'd married the woman his family had chosen.' Once again I could imagine exactly how that would happen.

Sarra also got married, to an English policeman called Neil Fotheringham. Tariq was about four at the time. Neil then adopted Tariq officially and they had the boy baptised as a Christian, assuming that Rashid was never going to accept that he was the boy's father. Sarra and Neil had then gone on to have three more children of their own. It was a family set-up very similar to my own, with one child from another relationship and then three from the marriage. I could picture it all too easily. I knew what a relief it was to find a man who was willing to treat all your children equally, and I also knew that you could never quite forget that there was another father involved.

'When Tariq was seven, I made contact with Rashid again,' Sarra continued. 'Even though we were very happy as a family unit, I felt an emotional need for him to identify himself as Tariq's father, for TT's sake as much as anything. It was obvious from his dark hair and olive skin that he had a different father to our other children, I thought he needed to establish his identity.

'Rashid wrote back and insisted on a DNA test to prove that Tariq was really his son. I suppose wealthy families are always getting paternity suits taken out against them and they probably just hand them over to their lawyers. I expect he hoped that a request like that would shut me up once and for all. Although I was insulted that he would suggest I was sleeping around and trying to fob him off with the bills, I could see that a DNA test would settle the matter once and for all, so we did it. The results proved I was telling the truth and that Rashid was TT's natural father. That changed everything.

'Suddenly Rashid had an interest in us. He announced he would like to meet his eldest son. By that time he had two boys and a girl with his wife, which had probably made him more aware of his responsibilities as a father. He told me that he'd informed his own father he had another grandson, which I can now see was very significant: the grandfather is very much the head of the Al-Habtoor family. I thought it was nice that Rashid and his father finally wanted to meet TT.'

Rashid, she said, came to England a few times to meet Tariq and then made Sarra an offer. He said that if she and Neil would like to move their family out to Dubai, the Al-

Habtoors would foot the bill, provide them with a house, find Neil a job as a fitness instructor and pay for the children to be privately educated.

'They said they wanted Tariq to experience his father's culture,' she said, 'and it seemed like a good opportunity for the whole family.'

The Fotheringhams took up the offer and all moved out to the booming, oil-rich state of Dubai to enjoy the ex-pat lifestyle. Rashid was as good as his word and took care of all the costs of settling them into their new home. Despite this enormous generosity from the Al-Habtoors, Sarra and Neil soon become dissatisfied with their new life, finding the house too small (it had only one servant's room, she informed me indignantly), and Tariq's father too demanding of his son's time.

'I was hardly getting to see TT at all,' she explained. 'He was always at his father's house.'

Neil found the job that had been arranged for him, which was as a recreation assistant in one of the Al-Habtoors' hotels, was not what he'd anticipated and became increasingly disillusioned with the whole situation. Nine months after arriving, Sarra decided she'd made a mistake and told Rashid that they wanted to return to England. By then, however, Rashid had bonded with his eldest son and didn't want to lose him again. He said that he was sorry they were not happy and he would do whatever he could to help them relocate back to England, but that he wanted Tariq to stay behind in Dubai with the family.

'Obviously I wasn't going to agree to that,' Sarra told me. 'But he'd made up his mind and he's a powerful man out there. At one point, I complained about the amount of time Tariq was spending with him, and pointed out that I hardly got to see my own son any more. Now he was saying that Tariq was his and kept him with him all the time. Neil and I couldn't get near him because he was always inside the house, which was heavily guarded. We went to the British embassy but they told us there was nothing they could do; the boy was with his father in his own country, it was all totally legal.'

As she finished telling me the story, her eyes full of tears, she seemed completely devastated to have lost Tariq and looked as if she didn't know how she would be able to live without the boy. It was a story I'd heard so many times by then that I had no reason to doubt anything she was saying. The events as she described them seemed to fit the pattern that I'd become so familiar with. She told me that once they got back to England they started court proceedings to win Tariq back, but that she was only allowed one phone call a week to the boy. I could imagine just how painful those calls must have been: trying to bond with a child who's 2,000 miles away in just a few minutes down a telephone line would be hopeless. Every time she hung up on him she must have felt a terrible despair at the thought it would be another week before she would hear his voice again.

'The courts told us that by taking Tariq to Dubai we'd given up his habitual residency in England. They said that only the courts in Dubai could decide on his future. But out there the

Al-Habtoors are all-powerful. They have more or less unlimited money. There was no way we could fight them on their own territory. Rashid was granted full custody.'

Later, when I was in Dubai, I was shown a marriage certificate purporting to belong to Rashid and Sarra.

'When you have a certificate signed by a Sheikh, there isn't much you can do to fight it,' she explained. 'And they don't recognise adoption out there, so Neil had no influence as Tariq's legally adoptive father in Britain. I was allowed to see Tariq under supervision for a few hours each day when I went out a couple of months ago, but now I'm back in England even my weekly phone calls have been stopped. I'm terrified he's slipping away from me. He's being taught Arabic and brought up in the Muslim faith.'

Despite her cut-glass accent and affectations she seemed a really nice young mother and I thought it would be a relatively straightforward mission to find the boy and get him out of Dubai and back to England. I told her I could see no reason why I couldn't help her. She seemed desperate to get started quickly. She showed me emails that Tariq had sent her, saying how much he wanted to come home. I noticed the boy said nothing nasty about his father or his life in Dubai, just the usual complaints of a young lad about any restrictions being put on him at the moment of writing, the sort of things that would be forgotten the next day, replaced by some new grumble. Sarra seemed to be reading a lot between the lines, but I had no reason to doubt that she was right. She was his mother, after all, she should have known better than anyone what he really meant by what he wrote.

Much of Tariq's writing was about a man called Adel, who Sarra told me was his 6ft 6in Moroccan bodyguard, which suggested that we were dealing with a family of some consequence. Adel, I discovered, had been hired specifically to ensure that Sarra didn't try to kidnap her son back. Getting him away from a full-time bodyguard was going to make things a little more difficult, but not impossible. It just meant we had to be extra careful with picking our moment to strike.

At the next meeting, Sarra's husband, Neil, came too. He was a traffic policeman and I didn't particularly take to him. He didn't appear to be very bright or to really understand what was going on. He seemed weak and very much under Sarra's influence. But I was growing to like Sarra more as I got to know her better, even though she acted a bit like a spoilt princess from time to time, and I had no reason to doubt the story she was telling. I agreed to help and we started to lay plans to get Tariq home to England. We decided to use Marlon's passport to get him out, since they were similar ages and of similar colouring and build. Neil knew about what we were doing but Sarra was the one making the decisions.

It seemed to me that the alarm was likely to go up pretty quickly with a family like the Al-Habtoors and they would be able to close the airports almost immediately. I had to come up with some alternatives to escaping by air. The plan that I favoured was for us to get Tariq and then for me to board a boat with him, which would take about two days to get us up to Iraq, from where we could get across the border into Jordan and back to England, a route with which I was now very familiar. I didn't think a family as rich as the Al-Habtoors, used to flying everywhere first class or in private planes, would expect us to leave by boat, a method of transport that was really only used by the less well-off. For as long as we were at sea we would be virtually invisible. Sarra would leave Dubai in the normal fashion, with no one stopping her since she wouldn't have Tariq with her. If they were aware of her movements, so much the better since they would be so busy watching her and trying to work out what she was up to that they would not be looking for us. She couldn't have got into Iraq anyway with Tariq and me, not being an Iraqi national. If she had been with us we would have been far more conspicuous and likely to be stopped. Sarra was not the sort of woman who melted easily into the background.

Sarra and Neil gave me $3,000, which I sent on to a contact in Iraq to arrange a safe exit for us over the border to Jordan. I wanted him to stay in a little hotel by the docks in Iraq until we got to him, and then travel up with us. That way we would look more like a normal family. As I had no idea when the actual snatch would take place he was going to have to stay there for at least a week, so the price of $3,000 was not excessively high.

Once the money was settled and the arrangements in Iraq were in place, Neil drove Sarra and me to Heathrow Airport.

'If you don't get him this time,' Neil told us, 'it doesn't matter, as long as you manage to make some contact with him.'

213

Although I could see what he meant, and understood that he was just trying to make Sarra feel less nervous, it occurred to me that he didn't know much about the way a mother's mind works to say that at the stage where she was hoping to bring her son home. Unfortunately, I could see the sense in what he was saying. I was pretty sure, however, that if we didn't get Tariq out on this trip we wouldn't get another chance. Once the Al-Habtoors were alerted to the fact that Sarra was trying to get him they would have bodyguards with him every second of every day. Our only chance was to act quickly and decisively.

We flew to Abu Dhabi so that the authorities wouldn't see our names coming into Dubai Airport. I couldn't be sure that the Al-Habtoors didn't have informers in passport control who would let them know if Sarra entered the country. I was hoping they weren't that suspicious of her yet, that they thought they had the situation under control, but I couldn't be sure and the risk wasn't worth taking. When we landed we hired a car and Sarra drove us down to Dubai. We checked into the Hilton and prepared ourselves.

'I need to see the house and spend some time watching their routine,' I told Sarra once we'd unpacked. 'So that we can work out the best time to get to him.' I intended to start the job as I had with most of the previous missions that had been successful. I was determined not to strike too soon and give away our presence in the country. We talked late into the night, too excited to fall asleep.

The following day she drove me out to what looked like a

fairly ordinary area of the city and pointed out a pleasant but unspectacular family house. It wasn't the sort of place I would have expected someone from a wealthy family to live in, but it still looked very comfortable. I wondered if perhaps she'd been overstating the wealth and importance of the Al-Habtoors.

'That's where Tariq's grandfather, the head of the family, lives,' she said, pointing to another, far more impressive house on the other side of the road. Obviously that was where the family power lay. The fact that the houses of the two generations were so close together fitted in with all my own experiences of how Arab families like to live. Just because Dubai is oil rich, the basic family values that I had encountered with Karim's and Mahmoud's families, and the many others that I had got to know over the years, remained unchanged. They might have traded simple village houses for comfortable urban mansions, but the concept of families staying in close proximity and presenting a united face to the outside world remained as strong as it always had been in that part of the world. I knew that we could not take on Rashid without taking on every other Al-Habtoor as well.

We spent two days in the car watching the comings and goings of the family between the house and the Emirates International School, where we knew Tariq was enrolled; it was the sort of routine that I'd grown so used to in the recent years that I felt almost comfortable with it. We would sit outside the front of the house for a while, and then drive round to the back when we felt we'd been there too long and might be arousing the suspicions of passers-by. I couldn't be sure that there weren't close-circuit cameras watching the area and didn't want to stay too long in any one place. We saw Rashid and the car coming and going with various members of the family, but we didn't see Tariq. We saw maids, chauffeurs and bodyguards driving to and from the house and the school with other children and we were sure that Tariq was in the car among them somewhere and that we were just missing seeing him each time. Considering the number of people we saw walking in and out of the house, it must have been quite crowded inside, but I assumed some of the staff were living in other neighbouring buildings.

Sarra knew that once a week, regular as clockwork, Tariq went to a particular internet café. We made sure we were there, waiting outside at the same time, but there was no sign of him. It was as if they knew we were coming and had deliberately changed his routine to outfox us. That made me uncomfortable. These people seemed to be better organised than the other families I'd been involved with.

'Maybe he's gone away for a bit,' I suggested.

It would be disappointing if we had to go all the way back home without even seeing him. We'd then have to arrange another trip which would increase the danger of being seen coming into the country, as well as increasing the costs for all of us.

'Maybe they're getting him into the school in secret somehow,' Sarra suggested.

'Let's try plan B then,' I suggested. 'I'll go into the school and make enquiries about sending my children there. I've done it a lot in the past. It always works.'

Sarra had been expressly forbidden from going into the school by the Al-Habtoor family. They owned it and were quite capable of enforcing any instructions they wanted. The staff had been informed what she looked like and told that on no account was she allowed to have access to Tariq. In fact the family were following all the rules that I gave to mothers who were afraid that their children were going to be snatched in England. But they hadn't reckoned on Sarra coming with an accomplice. They wouldn't be expecting me in there. As far as I knew they had no reason to connect me with Sarra or the family. I wouldn't arouse any suspicions. If I could get inside I could ascertain the layout of the classrooms, and find out where Tariq was likely to be at any particular time of the day. We could then work out the best way to snatch him without raising the alarm.

The next day Sarra drove me to within a few hundred yards of the school and parked. I got out of the car and walked towards the school. I noted there were guards on the gates but they didn't take any notice of a woman walking past. Why would they? There must be hundreds of mothers and teachers coming and going all day long. I went straight in and asked if I could be shown around the school, particularly Year Five, since that would be where my eldest son would be going if he joined the school. I said I'd like to meet the class teacher who would be in charge of my son. I told them I was moving to Dubai from Jordan. They very kindly took me around the whole school. It was a big place but I noticed the internal security seemed to be almost non-existent. I couldn't see any cameras and the doors didn't seem to be guarded, which was surprising considering how many wealthy and influential families sent their children there. They seemed to be relying completely on the guards at the gates.

The problem was there was the usual sea of children, virtually all of them dark haired and looking more or less identical as they rushed around from one place to another in their school uniforms. Even though I'd seen photographs of Tariq there was no way I would have been able to pick him out in such a fast-moving crowd; it would be like trying to pick out an individual ant in the midst of a nest.

The playgrounds were divided into year groups and Tariq's was near to the gate, which would make escape quicker if that was where we were going to snatch him. I could see that even if he was in the school, we'd never be able to get him out of any of the classrooms. They were too regimented, with a teacher in each room. Any other mother would be able to knock on a classroom door and ask to take their child out for some fictional dentist's appointment, but no teacher would allow Sarra to do that in the Al-Habtoors' own school. If we were going to take him from there it would have to be while he was playing outside. We would only have a few minutes to make our getaway, and it was here that the sea of dark heads seemed to be at its thickest and fastest moving. I stared at the children in despair. How would I ever find him if he was here? I would have to come back with Sarra, keep her face covered and hope that her maternal instincts would pick him out, even though she hadn't seen him for some months by then.

'I'm sure he must be in there somewhere,' I told her as I climbed back into the car. 'But I can't pick him out from all the others. We'll have to come back on Monday and you'll have to come in with me to point him out. The security's terrible, it won't be a problem if we get here while all the children are arriving and everyone is moving about, as long as we can separate him off from Adel. Once we know he's there we can plan how to get him out of the country quickly.'

On Monday we got up very early and drove back to stake out the school before the pupils started to arrive. Once the flow of cars had begun to build up and there were parents and children going in and out in sufficient quantities for us to be inconspicuous, Sarra drove us into the car park, past the security guards on the gate. We had decided we would attract much less attention in a car than on foot. No one seemed to be arriving at this school on foot.

We parked and got out of the car. We'd made some packed lunches and were carrying bundles of books so that it would look as if we were mothers with children at the school. We were both wearing complete black cover-up, so that our faces were hidden, only our eyes in view as they darted from side to side. I was sweating with a mixture of heat and nerves. Everything was a rush. We had to find him and act quickly. We wouldn't be able to do this too often. We dived in through the doors. We moved as fast as we could without drawing attention to ourselves, up and down staircases, along corridors and through crowds of children to all the places that had been pointed out to me the day before, desperately searching for a face that either of us might recognise.

There were five minutes until the bell would go for the start of school when we emerged into the playground for Tariq's year. We could see Adel, the bodyguard, on the other side having a surreptitious cigarette. He was a huge man in a leather jacket and t-shirt. He looked every inch the professional bodyguard, like a trained soldier in civilian clothes. I didn't fancy our chances of getting away if he spotted us. He obviously wasn't expecting any sort of trouble. He wasn't looking around, or even watching the children near him. He probably thought that with only a few minutes to go he would soon be able to relax until the end of the school day. Even professionals can be caught off guard occasionally.

'Where is he?' I whispered as we scanned the faces of the children nearest to him.

'I don't know,' Sarra hissed back through her veil. 'Maybe he isn't here.'

'He must be here,' I snapped.

'I can't see him!' I could hear a hint of panic in her voice and said nothing else.

We continued searching for what seemed like ages, while keeping half an eye on Adel, then Sarra turned her head and spotted some boys playing football in the furthest corner of the playground from him. They were all wearing the same navy blue shorts and blue and white shirts. To me they looked identical.

'There he is,' she said.

I glanced back at the bodyguard. He wasn't looking in our direction. To him we were just two more invisible women in a world full of such anonymous creatures. We'd had a lucky break and it threw me into a quandary. We might never get another chance as good as this, so should we take the boy now? Or would that be foolish? Would it be better to stick to the original plan and come back another day when we had the escape route all set up and knew exactly what we were doing? I only had a few seconds to make up my mind. Before I could say anything Sarra had forced the issue. She had gone over to her son and was bending down, lifting her veil so he could see her face. From where I was standing, Tariq didn't look as if he had a care in the world as he played with his friends. I moved in close behind Sarra so I could shield her from Adel, should he turn his head. The situation seemed to be taking on a momentum of its own and I had no choice but to go with it now she had exposed herself so blatantly.

'Hello, Sweet Pea,' she simpered, not making any attempt to hug or touch him. 'It's Mummy. You have to come with me.'

'I don't want to come with you, Mummy,' he said, his eyes darting nervously across to the bodyguard who was still blissfully unaware of what was going on. 'Daddy will be cross and Adel isn't with me. He has to be with me wherever I go.'

'Nonsense, TT,' she scolded. 'I'm your mother, you can come with me.'

I was surprised by the lack of physical affection between the two of them. With every other mother – child reunion I'd witnessed there had always been a lot of spontaneous hugging. The mothers always seemed to want to sniff the skins of their long-lost children, and they in turn seemed to want to weld themselves to their mothers. It was true that he was older than some of the others I'd been involved with, but he was the same age as Marlon and I knew how we would be clinging on to each other if we were in that situation.

'Come on, Sarra,' I muttered under my breath. 'Get him to the car.'

I glanced at my watch. There were only a couple of minutes to go before the bell would sound and the whole crowd would sweep into the building, leaving us fully exposed to Adel. We had to act quickly or not at all. I grabbed Tariq's arm.

'Get in the car now,' I hissed.

We almost lifted him off the ground between us and ran down the steps to the car park. Other children saw us running but no one raised an alarm. There were women and children and raised voices all around, and we didn't seem particularly out of the ordinary. Tariq was pulling against us but I knew we didn't have time to stop and coax him along. Together we were too strong for him and we bundled him into the back seat of the car, diving in after him.

Looking back now, or even a few minutes later, I could see that something wasn't right. I'd never had to force a child like that before and it felt all wrong, but I was so worried about being caught by Adel that I didn't stop to obey my better instincts. I was afraid I'd made a bad judgement, but it was too late now; we were committed to a course of action and couldn't go back. By now I'd realised that we were dealing with a seriously rich and powerful family. I could imagine that if there were bodyguards there could be guns involved and that made me doubly nervous after my experiences with Kate in Jordan. I wanted to get out of the country as quickly as possible, and worry about Tariq's reluctance to come once we were safely away. He was with his mother, after all, how bad could it be for him?

We laid him down on the seat and covered him up with a blue fleece. He kept protesting: 'Mummy, I've got to go back. You've got to take me back.'

'No, TT,' Sarra was saying. 'Your father's a very bad man. He took you from Mummy and you belong with me. We're going to go home to see Granddad.'

I was beginning to get a very bad feeling about the whole situation. I noted that she hadn't used talking to Neil as bait to coax him out of the school. I wondered if the bond between adoptive father and son was quite as strong as the two of them had been telling me. But I had more pressing problems to occupy my mind at that moment. Sarra was back behind the wheel of the car but she couldn't get through the school gates because all the other cars were leaving at the same time. The two security guards were watching every car that went past. We jerked backwards and forwards in our attempts to get to the front of the queue more quickly. I was terrified we would bump into one of the gleaming Mercedes or BMWs that were all around us, slowing down our escape and drawing attention to the car. Any moment now I expected to hear bells going off in the school and for Adel and others to come running out brandishing guns. I was desperate to get clear of the area as fast as possible.

I was also trying to plan what we should do next. The boat for Iraq left every Monday afternoon. In my mind originally I'd been thinking we would get the lie of the land this week, snatch the boy at the end of the week or even the following Monday, and catch the boat then. But now we would have to catch the one leaving that afternoon. There was no way we could stay in Dubai for a week once Tariq's father's family was looking for us. Nor did I fancy our chances of getting across a border or on to an international flight once the balloon had gone up.

We eventually reached the security guards and I held my breath, staring hard through the windscreen so as not to catch their eyes as we drove past. They didn't seem to be taking any notice of us at all as we edged our way forward amongst all the other parents and chauffeurs.

Suddenly we were past them and out on to the open road. I felt a weight lift off my shoulders – only for that one to be replaced by another. Tariq was getting louder, making a big fuss about wanting to get back to his father. We had to find a way to pacify him and I had to think about getting tickets for the boat as quickly as possible, in case the police started asking questions at the port.

'Let's ring Granddad in England,' Sarra said brightly, getting out her phone and dialling. 'He'd like to hear that you're coming home to see him.'

She made the call and Tariq spoke to his grandfather, but it didn't seem to make him feel any better. He was becoming more and more agitated at the thought of how angry his father was going to be. I needed to quieten him down so that I could think clearly. I also had to have him calm once we were boarding the boat, otherwise he would draw attention to us. I thought another man's voice might help, particularly if he could speak to him in Arabic, and rang Mahmoud to tell him the situation and to ask if he would have a word with Tariq.

Mahmoud was obviously worried to discover that we'd had to grab the boy with no immediate escape route set up, but he remained calm. I asked him to speak to Tariq and try to reassure him. I had a feeling that things were running out of my control and I was wishing Mahmoud was there to give me a few words of comfort too. He's always very good in a crisis.

They talked for a few minutes. When Tariq came off the phone he asked Sarra for his Gameboy and she passed it to him. He started playing and immediately seemed to be engrossed in whatever the game was. It seemed he was calming down.

'What time does the boat leave?' Mahmoud asked when I got the phone back from Tariq.

'Late this afternoon,' I said. 'I'm beginning to think we shouldn't wait around that long; that we should try to get to Qatar and fly out of there. The Dubai port and airport are likely to be the first places they'll be looking.'

'You'll have to go through a corner of Saudi to get to Qatar,' Mahmoud reminded me. 'You'd better hope they haven't closed the border by the time you get there.'

I knew now I was in more trouble than I'd ever been. I was up against a truly powerful family and there was a strong chance we could end up in jail. I hung up the phone, wishing Mahmoud was with me rather than 2,000 miles away, and concentrated on thinking.

'We need to get our stuff from the hotel before anything else,' I said. 'So we're ready to leave by whatever route we decide on.'

We drove back to the Hilton and I ran in, leaving Sarra and Tariq in the car. A small boy in a hotel lobby during school hours might have attracted attention, particularly if he started saying he wanted to go back to his father. In the bedroom I threw open our suitcases and crammed everything in as fast as I could, not stopping to worry about how creased it was all becoming. I lugged the cases down to the reception and paid the bill. Everything seemed to be taking forever. Why wouldn't people get a move on? I didn't want to say anything or become impatient, for fear of drawing attention to myself. I wanted to be as unmemorable as possible, just another anonymous Arab woman in a veil settling a bill. Finally the paperwork was completed and I went back out to the car with the bags. Sarra was still sitting in the driving seat and Tariq was engrossed in his Gameboy in the back. They didn't seem to be communicating at all. As she pulled away her phone went off. It was Neil.

'Don't worry, Sweet Pea,' she cooed at him. 'Everything's just fine. We'll be fine.'

I wondered if she was just being brave or whether she really thought we were now safe. Personally I was feeling extremely unsafe and being with someone who appeared not to have grasped the gravity of the situation did not help my confidence. It was a long drive. At one stage Sarra hit a bird. It made a surprising amount of noise as its feathers exploded past the speeding windows. The impact made Tariq jump and look up from his game. He was upset to see the broken corpse of the bird bouncing along the highway behind us. Sarra seemed rather impatient with his sentimental attitude, perhaps seeing it as a criticism of her driving.

'Looks like you've killed two birds with one stone,' I muttered and she gave one of her tinkling laughs.

When we reached the Saudi border we pulled over to wait and see if there was any unusual activity to indicate they were looking for us. We'd been travelling for hours with no breaks for food or drink. We hadn't even had a toilet stop. I felt bad enough, not having been able to face any breakfast before setting out that morning. I dreaded to think how poor little Tariq was feeling, but he wasn't complaining.

Sarra had been filling the boy's head with stories about how wicked his father was all the way from Dubai. 'He took you from your mummy,' she kept saying. 'No one should take a little child from their mummy.'

'Daddy doesn't talk badly about you, Mummy,' Tariq said in a puzzled voice. I don't think any child likes to hear their parents criticised by anyone, least of all by each other. After all, a child owes half its genes to its father and half to its mother, any criticism of either parent has to be a partial criticism of the child. I thought he was handling the situation in a very mature fashion for such a young boy.

I was glad of a chance to get out of the car at the border and get away from Sarra's voice for a few minutes as I tried to find out whether the border guards were going to be on the lookout for us yet. Trying to look casual, I fell into conversation in Arabic with a lorry driver who was resting in the shade, enjoying a cigarette and drink. I told him we were planning to get to Qatar Airport.

'Who's driving you?' he asked, looking around to see if there was a man with us.

'We're driving ourselves,' I replied uneasily.

'No.' He shook his head. 'They won't let you in. Women can't drive themselves in Saudi. If you want to fly to England you'll have to go back to Abu Dhabi Airport. Do you have visas for Qatar?'

'No.' I shook my head. I realised now we'd made a mistake. I shouldn't have allowed Sarra to rush me into grabbing the boy that morning. I'd forgotten women weren't allowed to drive in Saudi and now we'd wasted all those hours on the road. I'd also forgotten about the need for visas to get into Qatar. We'd enquired about them a few days before, just in case we needed them, but the authorities had said they would take four days to come. We still had all the paperwork for the applications with us.

'Then – ,' he shrugged as if he despaired of women's stupidity '– even if you got a lift across Saudi, you wouldn't be allowed into Qatar.'

'We're not going to be able to get out this way,' I told Sarra when I got back to the car. 'We're going to have to go back to the plan of escaping on the boat to Iraq. We'll have to drive back to the port and just hope they aren't watching it. It's possible they don't know he's gone yet; we might have a few more hours' leeway. We might just get there in time for the boat if we leave straight away.'

I climbed into the car and we headed back the way we'd come; still hungry and thirsty and now beginning to feel decidedly trapped inside the country. I couldn't believe I'd allowed us to get into such a dangerous situation. I was no longer sure I liked the idea of escaping with Tariq on my own if he wasn't keen to leave his father. As long as Sarra was there it wasn't my responsibility, but on my own I would have to face the fact that he didn't seem that anxious to return to England. If the boat trip was as uncomfortable as others I'd been on he was likely to be even less willing to co-operate after a few hours of rough sea.

'Where am I going?' Tariq asked at one stage.

'You're going to go to Iraq with Donya, and then fly on to England, Sweet Pea,' Sarra told him. 'And I'll fly home to meet you later.'

'We won't be flying economy, will we, Mummy? I have to go first class.'

I thought I'd better get business class tickets on the boat when we got there. I didn't want him kicking up a fuss over the standard of his accommodation when I was trying to melt into the background. I couldn't help wondering how he was going to survive living in a normal house in Camberley and going to a local school. It looked as if he might have been living the high life in Dubai for a little too long to be able to go back to his old life with any comfort.

We now had no choice but to keep moving as fast as possible. We were hungry and thirsty but we couldn't afford to take the time to get refreshments. As long as we were in the car and moving I felt strangely safe. I was beginning to dread having to get out and stop being an anonymous woman in the back of a car. We headed back across the rocks and sands of Abu Dhabi towards Dubai and Port Rashid. All three of us were becoming tired and short-tempered with one another. I was also deeply frightened, and puzzled by the fact that Sarra didn't seem to be in the least perturbed by our increasingly perilous position. The longer we were in the country the greater the chances that they would manage to close all means of escape and tighten the net around us. It was as if she took it for granted that we were going to get away. Neil kept phoning her and dishing out advice on what we should be doing. He was beginning to get on my nerves. What the hell did he know, sitting back there in England while we drove desperately around the desert looking for a way to escape?

We arrived at Port Rashid about an hour before the boat for Iraq was due to leave. That suited me. I wanted to be able to walk straight on to the boat and disappear into a cabin. Everything looked peaceful with dockside business going on as usual. There were no roadblocks or extra security people in evidence.

I began to feel more optimistic. Perhaps we still had enough time before the alarm was raised. Maybe they still hadn't noticed that he'd gone. They'd realise quickly enough at the end of the school day when the car came to pick up him and Adel.

'Drop me at the ticket office and you keep circling around with Tariq until I come out,' I said. 'I'll get the tickets and take Tariq straight on to the boat and you can go to the airport and get the first flight out to anywhere.'

Sarra did as I suggested and I went into the building to get the tickets. No one seemed to be paying me any special attention. I was, after all, just another veiled woman, totally anonymous. As I came back out into the hot sun I saw Sarra driving towards me, having been around the block. She pulled up at the kerb and I opened the back door to allow Tariq to get out. As he wriggled across the seat towards me I was suddenly surrounded by plain-clothes policemen in traditional Arab dress. Their leader showed me his identity card and arrested us in the name of the rulers of Abu Dhabi and Dubai. I felt as if my legs were going to give out beneath me. For the first time ever I'd been caught in the act. After all the years of imagining this moment and the horrors that were bound to follow, it had arrived and I felt sick with fear.

I also now had serious doubts about whether I'd been doing the right thing in helping Sarra to take Tariq away from his father. At no stage in the long car journey had the boy bonded with his mother and he'd repeatedly said that he wanted to go back to Rashid. I had a feeling I'd made a terrible mistake and was about to pay the price. I felt more frightened than I'd ever felt in my life before. This was worse than being chased around Amman by armed men, because this time there was no chance of escape.

'Oh my goodness,' I joked, in a last-ditch attempt to laugh my way out of the situation. 'Is this *Candid Camera*?' But I knew it was no television stunt. Sarra had got her phone out. 'Who are you calling?' I asked.

'Neil,' she said. 'He's a policeman, he can do something.'

'Never mind Neil,' I snapped. 'There's nothing he can do to help now. Phone the British embassy.'

The police showed no glimmer of humour at the situation, escorting us from the car to the police station within the port buildings. I noticed, with relief, that they weren't searching the car for our bags and papers, many of which would have proved that we'd been planning this whole operation from the start. It would be much better if we could say that we'd just gone to visit the boy, with no intention of kidnapping him. With any luck we'd be able to convince them that Sarra had been overcome with maternal emotions upon seeing Tariq at the school and we now realised we'd made a mistake, which we deeply regretted. It didn't sound very convincing, even in my head, but it seemed like our best chance.

Inside the police station everyone was talking around us but no one was explaining what was happening. Phone calls were being made and we were being ordered to wait whenever we said anything. My fears were becoming almost uncontrollable and every so often I would be unable to stop a little cry coming out when I thought of what lay in store. It seemed likely that we were going to go to jail for this and I realised that I might not be able to see my children for years.

The thought made me cold with panic. Would they forget about me in that time? I wished with all my heart that Mahmoud was standing there with me, putting his arm around me, calming me down. I don't know what else he could have done, but at least he would have known I loved him. I imagined him at home, just getting on with the daily routine of taking the children back and forth to school, cleaning their clothes, keeping their stomachs full and making sure their homework was done, blissfully unaware of the mess their mother had got herself into. I wished with all my heart I was there with them.

Once the initial panic was over and they realised we weren't going to cause any trouble, the uniformed police were kind to us, offering us tea and talking to us as if we were no more than casual visitors to their station, but the plain-clothes ones who'd arrested us continued to act aggressively, as if they were suspicious of what we would do next.

It seemed they were expecting someone important to arrive and deal with us, but no one would tell us who. They just kept on telling us to wait. When Tariq's father and grandfather arrived it was obvious that I'd underestimated their power right to the end. The grandfather was evidently an enormously respected man, which you could see from the way the police reacted to him. They were both wearing traditional robes and seemed immensely nice men. I was now pretty sure that I'd acted too quickly in taking up Sarra's cause without doing some investigations of my own.

The Al-Habtoors were obviously men of substance. I already knew the family was rich and powerful because of what Sarra had told me, but I would soon read even more. They were an old trading family with investments all over the world. Rashid was reputed to have played polo with Prince Charles and was believed to be friends with people as varied as Prince Michael of Kent, Omar Sharif and Jean-Claude Van Damme. They had huge homes all over the world, including England, and Rashid's brother had once gone out with supermodel Naomi Campbell. They'd recently bought Monkey Island on the Thames, which contained a 150-year-old country house hotel and they owned other major hotels in Egypt, Dubai, the Lebanon and Jordan. They had a fleet of executive jets that transported business people around the world. Their planes were all filled with state-of-the-art communications equipment. They also owned a car-rental company, which provided Rolls-Royces, Bentleys and Aston Martins to clients. Their property portfolio included apartment complexes in Dubai and a number of cinema and entertainment complexes around the United Arab Emirates and numerous other luxury developments. Their engineering companies were responsible for most of the projects in Dubai in the recent years of the building boom, which has created one of the most impressive modern cities in the world. They owned their own stables and international standard polo club and hosted an annual international tennis challenge competition. They also owned a publishing company producing books and magazines. Overall they employed around 6,000 people. This family truly did have access to unlimited resources.

'Come.' Rashid gestured to Tariq to go to him.

'You're not having him,' Sarra snapped, sticking her chin out defiantly.

'We must leave the boy with the mother for the moment,' the senior police officer said, with the utmost respect, 'while we find out the custodial situation.'

Tariq's father bowed his head in acquiescence. He did not attempt to argue or raise his voice in anger. He seemed confident that matters would sort themselves out if allowed to run their course. I had always believed that she had full custody of Tariq. Over the next hour it became obvious that the Dubai authorities did not agree. They didn't seem to think she had any right to her son at all.

She and I and Tariq were transferred by car from the port to the main police station in the town. The father and grandfather travelled in another car and there was a convoy of police cars to escort us: sirens blaring and lights flashing as we roared through the streets, making heads turn.

Sarra and I were interrogated for nine gruelling hours until I felt ready to faint from exhaustion. My eyes and head were throbbing with tiredness as I struggled to find the right answers to their endless questions. Because Sarra didn't speak Arabic it was all done in English, but written up in Arabic. Although I speak the language I can't read it, and so I had no idea what I was signing at the end of the ordeal. I didn't care. I would have signed anything at that stage. They weren't unkind to us. They let us have drinks, but they were determined to get to the bottom of what we thought we were up to in their country. I think they were nicer to me than Sarra because I was a Muslim and spoke to them respectfully. She gave the appearance of talking down to everyone.

We told them that nothing had been planned, that it had just been the spontaneous action of a mother who loved her child. But in my bag lay the application forms we'd filled in for visas for Qatar, the maps and all the other paperwork that we'd collected in the preceding weeks while planning our escape from Dubai. Afraid that they would eventually search our bags, I took the opportunity of slipping the paperwork out when my interrogator left the room for a few minutes, and slid them down the back of his desk, tucking them out of sight. As far as I know they're still there.

They'd separated us for the interrogation so that we couldn't compare notes, but we'd agreed previously that if we did get caught we would stick to the same story about it not being a planned kidnapping. It was obvious they didn't believe us.

After that nine hours they made their decision regarding Tariq, taking him away and returning him to his father. Things were not looking good for us, and we were moved to another police station. When we arrived there we were taken into a private room together and told what we were going to be facing.

'You –' the police spokesman pointed at Sarra ' – are being charged with kidnapping. You – ' he pointed to me, ' – are charged with being accessory to kidnapping.'

I couldn't understand how Sarra could remain so cool about the whole thing. I could see we were on our way to jail but she just seemed to be carrying on as if the whole thing was no more than a temporary inconvenience, like having her credit card turned down on a shopping expedition. Something that could be cleared up the moment her husband showed up or once a few phone calls had been made to the right people.

'We're in big trouble, here,' I said when we were on our own together.

'Don't worry,' she said in her most superior voice, 'Neil will deal with it.'

Having met Neil I didn't think he had the ability to deal with a traffic offence in Tooting, never mind a kidnapping charge in Dubai.

'The press in England will be in uproar,' she went on cheerfully. 'They'll get us out.'

I couldn't imagine that the press would be in uproar at all. And if they were I didn't think that the Dubai authorities would give a damn what was happening in England. It all seemed a very long way away from that sparse, uncomfortable little room.

We were taken downstairs to the cells, relieved of all our money, jewellery and other possessions and directed to sit in a small concrete room with barred doors. It was spartan but very clean, with a tiny kitchen attached. There were two large Arab women, one of them wearing a lot of make-up, already in the room, chattering to each other about us as we came in. When I answered them in Arabic they seemed surprised and backed off. They already knew all about what we were being accused of and watched us with interest as we talked to each other in English.

'You will stay here for 10 minutes,' a policeman told us, and the doors clanged shut behind him. The minutes kept on ticking by.

An hour later they came back and told us we could buy phone cards to call our families. I rang Mahmoud. I explained quickly what was happening, not sure how long my money would last.

'Look after the children,' I said. 'I think I'm going to be here for quite a long time. Don't contact anyone. There's nothing they can do from England. It'll have to be done from this end.'

'OK,' he said, his voice as calm as always but sad. 'I love you.'

'I love you too,' I said. 'Kiss the children for me.'

The full horror of the situation struck me when I heard his voice. I'd never been away from any of my children for more than a few weeks and now I didn't know when I would see them again. It might not be for years. I knew I'd been rash in accepting the job without looking into it further, and now I was going to pay the price for my hotheadedness. Up till now I'd been lucky, but my luck had just run out. I started to cry, imagining my children's faces and the little night-time rituals we all had. I thought of all the times I'd shouted at Marlon for not doing his homework and regretted every one of them, or the times I got cross with him for still being on his computer at 10 o'clock at night when he should have been asleep. He was such a good boy. And Khalid, my clever little future doctor, with his delicate health and need for constant attention. Then there was the angelic, curly-haired Amira. I remembered the numbers game we would play, where she would hold my hand with her tiny, plump fingers and squeeze it once, I would squeeze back twice, she three times and so on until she was squealing with laughter. And then there was Alla, the smallest child and the biggest handful of them all with his loud voice and cheeky ways.

The 10-minute wait grew into a whole night and I cried myself to sleep on the dirty mattress, wondering if I would ever see them all again.

The next day we were moved to new holding cells while they processed more paperwork. These cells were off a long corridor with a toilet at the end. Behind every door there were other prisoners, about thirty of us in all. There were no windows to let in any light or to let out any of the cigarette smoke, which choked up the hot, stale, sweaty air. There was one small television in the corner of one of the rooms, which flickered shrilly to itself.

As we got to know our cellmates we discovered they were from a wide variety of nations: Russian, Romanian, English, Bosnian. Many of them were hookers, all pleasant women who seemed to be resigned to their fate.

There was one red-haired English woman called Vicky who said she was in for drug-related crimes. I spent a lot of time talking to her in order to get away from Sarra's voice. We quickly became good friends.

'You'll go in front of the public prosecutor,' she explained, 'and he'll decide what's going to happen to you, what you're going to be charged with.'

At that every woman in the room started chipping in with advice about which public prosecutor was the best to get and which ones were the real demons. This was the world they lived in, their fates decided seemingly arbitrarily by this official or that. A brush with a kind official could mean their lives were restored to them, coming up against a man who decided to teach them a lesson could mean they stayed incarcerated for periods that seemed to them indefinite. It was like listening to schoolchildren talking about which teachers were the strictest and which were the most likely to take a lenient view of some minor infringement of the rules.

'The worst one is the chief prosecutor,' one of them said. 'He's really tough.' There were shouts of agreement from all round. Everyone seemed to have had some sort of a problem with this monster of a man. The way our luck was going it seemed inevitable that we would end up in front of him. I felt myself give an involuntary shiver at the prospect.

'They're never in any hurry to sort you out,' Vicky went on. 'I've been in here four months and I haven't even been seen yet. I'm probably facing a 10-year sentence. By the time they actually get round to doing the sentencing I'll probably have served the time.'

They all had their stories to tell. There was one prostitute who'd already been given two years, and another woman who'd been locked up for doing nothing more than having an illegitimate baby. Their crimes didn't seem like anything compared to what we were in for. If the authorities doled out sentences like that for things that weren't even crimes in England, they were going to throw away the key for a couple of kidnappers. All day long we listened to these stories and by the next evening I could see Sarra was beginning to grasp the severity of our situation at last. When the lights went out we huddled together on a mattress on the floor like a couple of scared children and managed to fall asleep until six o'clock the following morning when they woke us all up to face another day. The moment I opened my eyes I felt choked by the smell of stale smoke and perspiration.

Later that morning Sarra was called upstairs to speak to a woman called Suzanne who was from the British embassy. She was up there for an hour and a half as I sweated away downstairs, wondering what was happening, praying they hadn't managed to talk her into confessing that the whole trip had been planned with the intention of bringing Tariq back to England.

'Everything's going to be fine,' Sarra assured me when she came back into the cells with her old breeziness restored. I had to admire her ability to bounce back in adversity. I felt a glimmer of optimism.

It was my turn next. Suzanne from the embassy was a beautiful woman with long hair down to her waist, but the thing I noticed most about her was that she smelled so fresh and fragrant after the stale stench of the cells. She wasn't the only person I was meeting for the first time. I was also confronted with the head of human rights from the police station where we were being held: a huge, fat man with a dark bushy beard. He didn't seem at all hostile and my spirits continued to rise. Maybe this ordeal was going to be over quicker than I'd feared.

'I need to contact my family,' I said when Suzanne introduced herself. 'I need you to send some money to make sure they're OK.'

'I'll see to that,' she assured me. 'Is there anything else you need?'

There were some things but they were still in the car and I didn't want anyone to be rifling through there because they'd find the other pieces of paper, which would show that Sarra and I had planned the whole thing from the beginning.

'It's OK,' I said quickly. 'I'm fine.'

'There's been a lot of publicity in England,' Suzanne told me. 'It's been all over the papers.'

I felt my optimism lurch. Did that mean that Neil had spilled the beans about all our planning meetings? It might be good to have someone stirring up public opinion in our favour, but not if it meant incriminating us.

'Has he?' I asked cautiously, not wanting to give anything away myself.

'You're going to be charged with kidnapping,' the fat man interrupted, probably not interested in anything that might be going on so far away from Dubai. 'You could face three years in jail.'

'But Sarra's just told me everything's going to be fine,' I

protested, realising how foolish my words sounded as I said them.

'I don't know what planet she's living on,' Suzanne said, shaking her head despairingly. 'It's most likely you will both be charged.'

'OK,' I tried to take the news in. I could feel tears welling up and I turned to Suzanne again. 'If I go to jail can you just stay in touch with my family and make sure they're OK?'

'Of course,' she said. 'It's in the papers over here too. They're calling you a professional kidnapper, and they're asking how you managed to get the child away from a trained bodyguard. There's all sorts of speculation. Some people are saying that he was in league with you. There are stories on the internet about how you packed Tariq up in a box and stored him in the boot of the car.'

Despite the gravity of the situation I couldn't stop a guffaw of laughter from escaping. Both Suzanne and the human rights man joined in for a moment at the prospect of Sarra and me trying to cram Tariq into a box against his will under the eyes of the guards, before we returned to the serious business at hand.

My interview didn't take as long as Sarra's and then I was back downstairs in the cells again. Sarra didn't ask me any questions about what had gone on. I think she was trying to block out the reality of the situation so she could continue living in her dreamland for a bit longer. I didn't bother to disillusion her. I was too busy trying to absorb everything I'd been told. The others didn't ask many questions either, as they could probably see from the look on my face that I hadn't been given any good news.

An hour or two later we were moved yet again. This time it wasn't to another police station, it was to a full-scale jail. We travelled in closed vans along with all the other women we'd been sharing with. The police tried to cheer us up, telling us the place we were going to had a garden, and Vicky told us she'd heard it was a nice place. To me it felt like we were travelling further and further away from the world I knew, into some dark labyrinth of ever more terrible jails, with my home and family becoming a more and more distant memory. When we rolled up at the gates and actually saw where we were going our spirits plummeted even further. It looked like Fort Knox. As we made our way in the doors banged behind us and the keys rattled and clanked.

'Time to check in at the Dubai Hilton,' I joked weakly as they went through the formalities of registering us. I was hoping that we'd be staying in one place from now on. I was feeling tired and my back was aching from bumping and crashing about in the back of a van. The more places we were moved to the more difficult it would be for people to find us and help us and the easier it would be for them to forget we existed. At that moment I couldn't imagine that anyone could possibly save us from the fate that was awaiting us.

I was getting on well with Vicky by that stage and she came in to share a cell with Sarra and me and a Filipino lady who we also got on with. The Filipino had been a live-in domestic and had got into some sort of trouble with the family that was employing her. She didn't say exactly what the trouble was and I didn't feel inclined to ask. In a situation like that, if someone didn't volunteer information about themselves it seemed prudent to mind your own business. I was determined to keep cheerful and kept up the jokes about us all being on holiday. There was a good spirit in the group, which only partially masked the fear and sadness at the situation we'd all got ourselves into. The captain who was running the jail was a woman, and she was very sweet to us, saying that she didn't believe we should have been sent there for what we'd done. She seemed regretful that she had to lock us up but the decision was obviously out of her hands.

The cell had a pair of bunks on each side but no blankets or pillows. There was no other furniture, nowhere to put our clothes or possessions. It stank of the men who'd been there for years before it was converted to a women's prison. I bagged a bottom bunk, not wanting to be clambering up and down with my bad back and Sarra took the top one. I lay down on the dirty mattress and stared up at the slats above. I noticed lots of tiny little balls of rolled up paper stuck to the slats. There were about 400 of them and I realised they were the way in which a previous inmate had marked off the days of his or her sentence. It seemed a good idea but I didn't have any paper to roll up so I just pushed one to the side, like a bead on an abacus. The next day I pushed another. It seemed as though a lot more were going to be moved.

The conditions in the prison were hard. We stayed in our cells all the time, except when we were taken to another windowless concrete room to eat. The food was inedible and I couldn't bring myself to force any of it down. I was too tense and nervous and desperate for fresh air. We hadn't been given any cutlery so if we wanted to eat any of the stews they put in front of us we had to use our fingers. I didn't have a mug either but Vicky let me share hers. The showers and toilets were at the end of the corridor and didn't look as if they'd ever been cleaned. Sarra couldn't get over the fact that most of them didn't have doors and that there was no privacy. I couldn't bring myself to use them, especially once I saw the prostitutes using them when they were brought in during the night and I became frightened of what I might catch. Once a day we could have showers, so I would empty my bladder into the drain then, and hold on for the rest of the day, which wasn't hard considering how little I was drinking.

To have a shower you had to be something of a contortionist because you had to keep pressing against a button on the wall to keep the water flowing, and hold the door shut at the same time as washing yourself. I worked out that if I pressed my backside against the button and my foot against the door that left my hands free to do the actual washing.

Although the women warders were quite kind to Sarra and me they were very intimidating to any of the other women who didn't understand Arabic. Their uniforms were like army clothes but they all wore the most enormous amounts of make-up and spent the whole time arguing and joking amongst themselves in shrill, aggressive voices. They were amazingly inefficient and could make a roll-call of thirty people last half an hour. They found the fact that I was a Muslim and spoke their language fascinating. It was a great advantage.

Everything was concrete and painted white, which became incredibly monotonous on the eye. There were no windows in any of the walls. We were entirely cut off from all the sights and sounds and smells of the outside world. The little garden we'd been promised turned out to be no more than another cell with a high metal grill instead of a roof, so that you could look through at the cloudless blue sky and get a sniff of fresh air, but the heat of the sun turned it into an oven.

A man from the British embassy came to visit us in the night with his wife. He was very camp, with long fingernails and a perfect tan. I liked him. He seemed like a last tenuous link with our previous lives. He told us to let him know if there was anything we wanted. What I wanted was to get back to my family, wrap them in my arms and never let them go.

'Could you get us some toothpaste and a towel?' I asked.

My mouth was beginning to taste disgusting. We'd got all the toiletries we needed in the car but I still didn't want to give anyone the idea of searching through them. He came back later with a collection of the sort of miniature toothpastes you get given when you stay in hotels. He also produced one hard, stiff little towel. I felt sure there must be some international convention about the basic necessities that prisoners should be given, regardless of their crime or the country they're imprisoned in, but I didn't say anything. I was grateful for any small improvement in our conditions at that stage and didn't want to acquire a reputation at the embassy as a troublemaker.

The next day Sarra and I were tightly handcuffed, marched out to another van, and told we were being taken up in front of the public prosecutor. Once again we were being bumped around like goods on the way to market. On the way we stopped at the police station where we'd previously met the human rights man, the large man with the bushy beard. I asked to see him and was taken in.

'Listen,' I said, not feeling I had much to lose by this stage. 'There are no blankets, no pillows and there's no fresh water for the prisoners where we are. If things don't improve I'm going to be talking to the press. Those women aren't being properly looked after.'

He appeared surprised by the information and then he smiled. I could tell I'd got through to him. He seemed like a nice man and I felt he might just do what I asked.

'You're a lovely person,' he said very sweetly. 'I'll look into these matters for you.'

The encounter made me feel a little bit more hopeful about our plight as we were then bundled back into the van to continue on our way to the public prosecutor's office. At least some people in authority out here didn't think I was an evil kidnapper, stealing children for my own nefarious purposes. The journey seemed to take forever as the driver and guards stopped every few miles to buy themselves bottles of water and watermelons to refresh themselves. No one offered us anything, but then we were prisoners. In the end we arrived late, only to find that the British media were already there, including a team from *Tonight With Trevor McDonald*, but they'd been put in a holding cell for three hours while they waited for us, which hadn't improved their mood. I felt quite hopeful at the sight of them; they were like another lifeline back to Britain. It showed we hadn't been completely forgotten. It also made me nervous. Would the presence of the British media aggravate the Dubai authorities? Would they feel that they had to make an example of us in the eyes of the outside world?

We were bustled through to see the prosecutor and who did we get? The chief! The one everyone had warned us about. Sarra was taken into his office first and I was made to wait outside. She was in there for what seemed like hours and when she came out, wide-eyed and dazed, we weren't allowed to speak before I was taken in. At first glance he didn't look quite such a monster as he was painted. He was dark skinned with gold-rimmed glasses and dirty teeth. He was not big but he was still intimidating because of the intensity of his manner. As soon as he started to speak I realised why everyone dreaded coming up in front of him.

I've never met someone who was able to make me shake with the sheer power of his stare, but this man did. He seemed to brim over with anger. He was the one they said would want to make an example of us, particularly me, the woman who, in his eyes, dared to snatch children away from their fathers, someone with no respect for the laws that he represented and believed in passionately.

The little man from the embassy was there to act as a translator. They obviously didn't realise I understood Arabic and I'd decided not to let on. This man was succeeding in frightening me into silence, a feat not many people have ever been able to achieve. He held my life in his hands, or at least the next few years of it. As she walked past me, Sarra still seemed to be acting as if she knew everything was going to be all right. I felt like I was fighting for my life.

'Ask her how she would feel if she was the father and someone came and stole her child from her?' the prosecutor demanded.

'I'd be pretty angry,' I replied in Arabic, not waiting for the translation, too impatient to speak up for myself to be able to bide my time. 'But why did he steal the child from the mother in the first place?'

'She understands Arabic, this girl?' He raised his shoulders in a questioning gesture to the man from the embassy.

'Yes, I understand Arabic,' I snapped.

'How come?'

'I'm married to an Iraqi,' I replied. I didn't think he needed any more information about my past than that.

'How many times have you done this before?' Now he was speaking to me directly.

'Never,' I lied. 'I help women to make contact with their children, but I've never done this before.'

I would have loved to tell him exactly what I'd done in the past and to explain why I was proud of it and why I would do the whole thing again if I had a chance. But at that moment I was so terrified of being separated from my children for the next three years that I succeeded in holding my tongue. The interrogation went on for a long time and at one stage the man from the embassy went out to speak to Sarra. A man from the public prosecutor's office came back in with him, accusing him of telling Sarra what was going on, helping us to corroborate one another's stories. There was an angry exchange of words. Tempers were rising. He seemed to see the whole thing as a conspiracy to embarrass the Dubai authorities.

'She told me this was all your fault,' the prosecutor said, nodding his head in the direction of the door to show he meant Sarra.

'If she did then she's lying,' I replied, pretty sure that Sarra would never have said such a thing. The night before in the cell we'd gone through exactly what we were going to say yet again, rehearsing each other until we were sure we'd be telling the same story no matter how long they separated us for or how many trick questions they sprang on us. Other people had told us that he liked to try to trick people and turn them against one another, so we were ready for him.

The interrogation seemed to go on forever and I began to wonder if he was planning to keep me there until I couldn't stand any more and agreed to whatever he said, just to get away. Eventually he fell silent, writing notes for a while and then sitting back and staring at me with his unnerving eyes.

'Very well,' he said. 'I am willing to allow you out on bail until your trial. But we will be keeping your passports and if you attempt to leave Dubai by any illegal means you will be back in the jail and you will not be coming out.'

Although we still had to face the prospect of going back inside to serve our three years, or whatever sentence we were to be given, at least we were getting out of jail for the moment and would be able to sleep in decent beds, take decent showers and eat decent food. I would also be able to make contact with Mahmoud and the children on a regular basis. I was desperate to hear their voices and assure them that I was all right. If we were outside the jail we could be talking to people, putting our story to the media and to anyone else who would listen, and working to get the case against us dismissed. It was a big step forward, but we still weren't home. If we were tried and found guilty we'd be back inside for a long stretch.

There was one more bridge to cross before we could actually become even temporarily free. For us to get out of the jail, someone else had to surrender their passport alongside ours, as a guarantee that we wouldn't skip the country. The public prosecutor wasn't planning to take any chances with us at all.

'Who can we get to do that for us?' I asked Sarra when we were told, imagining that I might still have to spend the next few months in the cell simply because no one would come forward with a passport.

'Don't worry,' Sarra said brightly, 'I have a friend, Jackie, who'll do that for us.'

She gave the authorities her friend's address. Jackie was contacted, and we waited and waited at the public prosecutor's office. Jackie didn't appear. In the end the authorities decided she wasn't coming and we were sent back to jail for the night. We had to hope that she would turn up the next day.

As we were taken down the other women in the cells started

to applaud us and cheer. I couldn't understand it. Were they clapping because we'd managed to get bail, or at least we would have if we could find someone with a passport? Were they sympathising because they knew we'd had to spend the day pitted against the dreaded chief prosecutor? I soon realised why they were so happy. My tirade at the police station that morning had worked and we'd been given fresh sheets, blankets and pillows. Everything in the block had been cleaned. It was like a different place. I felt a surge of grateful affection for the burly human rights man. It seemed he had taken note of what I'd said. The prison warden welcomed us back and explained that my words had hit their mark. She seemed as grateful as the inmates themselves.

Sarra was trying hard to remain her usual cheerful, optimistic self, despite the fact that her friend hadn't turned up, and that it looked as if we were going to have to spend another night in jail. I warmed to her more than I had in the previous few days. I knew from what I'd heard before we were separated that she'd stood up to the public prosecutor well, showing a lot of courage and I admired that. I could see she was nearing the end of her tether and that being let down by her friend was pretty much the last straw, although she would never have admitted it.

'It's going to be all right,' I said, in the hope of comforting her, and she burst into tears. The full horror of our situation seemed to have finally got through to her and she wasn't able to keep up her normal cheerful façade any longer.

Jail was harder for her than me. Because she didn't speak

Arabic she'd kept herself slightly separate from the other women, which must have made her feel lonely. I think they all believed she didn't mix because she felt she was better than them and they hadn't taken to her as a result. She seemed isolated.

At midnight, just after we dropped off to sleep, we were woken again by a jangling of keys and loud voices. We were out, they told us. Someone had bailed us and surrendered their passport. I wondered if the mysterious Jackie had turned up after all, but when we reached the front desk we discovered it was the *Trevor McDonald* team who'd come to our rescue. I felt a huge surge of affection for the great British media. One of the television production team, a guy called Nigel, had given up his passport for us and come up with the bail money. I thought that was the most magnificent gesture and I was very touched.

As we headed back to the hotel I realised how ill I felt. I'd barely eaten a thing for three days and felt weak with hunger and with the adrenaline of fear. Every muscle in my body ached from lying on the uncomfortable mattresses and sitting on hard benches. We hadn't changed our clothes in days either and I couldn't wait to shower and put on some clean things.

We were taken to the luxurious Trade Centre Hotel and were checked into a room. Now the media was in town no expense was going to be spared in keeping us comfortable while our tale unfolded for their viewers and readers around the world. The hotel room was a dramatic contrast to the cells we'd inhabited over the previous days. The first thing we did was make ourselves a cup of tea.

Now, as we sat in the luxurious room sipping hot tea from a clean cup, it was my turn to burst into tears. The strain of the whole operation suddenly overwhelmed me and the kindness and concern of the television crew was just too much to bear. I also had difficulty adjusting to sitting in a hotel room having a cup of tea while Vicky and the others were still stuck in their cells. Because I hadn't had a change of clothes Vicky had lent me some of hers, which I immediately sent to the hotel dry cleaners on our release so that I could return them to her. It always amazes me how generous people are when they have virtually nothing to spare.

I immediately rang Mahmoud to find out how the children were. I could tell I'd woken him and it took a few seconds for him to focus his thoughts. He told me they were fine, although Khalid was a little under the weather again. I felt a stab of guilt at not being there for him. I couldn't help wondering if Mahmoud was not telling me everything in order to spare me from worry, which made me worry all the more. He also told me he was getting a lot of pressure from the newspapers. They were offering him thousands of pounds to tell his story, and they were even offering to fly him out to Dubai so he could be with me. It would have been great to have had him there, dealing with the journalists and the phone calls for me, and just giving me a comforting cuddle when I needed it, but I knew he wouldn't leave the children at a time like this and I was grateful to him for that. I was nervous about what the British media might do now. I didn't want them printing anything that would upset the public prosecutor.

'They're asking if it's true that you've done this sort of thing before,' he said. 'They've heard rumours about the other missions. They've even been turning up at the kids' school. Some of the other mothers you've helped have been on television saying what a good person you are and how you have a heart of gold.'

'Don't say anything to any newspapers,' I said, feeling an increasing sense of panic. 'If the public prosecutor out here starts hearing stories through the British media about how this was all planned he'll be locking us up and throwing away the key.'

He promised to stay quiet and to kiss the children for me. I promised to ring back to speak to them when they were awake. There was a lot going on at home that I didn't find out about until later. My sister, Sandra, had done an amazing job of rallying the family round, bringing my aunts and uncles down from Scotland to stay with her in London so that they could all help Mahmoud with the children. On one call Mahmoud told me how proud he was of Marlon for handling himself with such amazing maturity and dignity under pressure, even answering the phone to journalists and giving exactly the right answers to their questions. One morning he was interviewed by *GMTV*, who were being very supportive of us and very gentle with Mahmoud and the children.

'Do you miss your mum?' the interviewer asked him.

'What child wouldn't miss their mother?' he replied, looking at her with those big, dark, grave eyes of his. I felt so proud when I heard about it.

Children have their own way of dealing with stress and worry. Mahmoud explained the situation to all of them right from the beginning and checked they understood what was going on, in case other children at school told them wild, inaccurate stories or they were caught unawares by an unscrupulous journalist. They then gave every appearance of blocking it from their minds and never spoke about it again, just getting on with their lives and waiting for me to come back. I guess they knew there was nothing they could do and so they just allowed themselves to rely on the grown-ups to sort everything out. If only we were as infallible and all-powerful as our children like to believe.

They might not have been saying anything about the situation, but I'm certain it must have been in the back of all their minds all the time. One evening, after having got them all into bed, Mahmoud was sitting downstairs watching the television news to see if there was any word about our situation, when he heard the sound of little feet and Amira appeared at the bottom of the stairs.

'Is Mummy OK now?' she asked sleepily.

'Yes,' Mahmoud assured her, 'Mummy is OK.'

'She just came to see me,' Amira said, allowing her father to scoop her up and take her back upstairs to return to her dreams.

If he had told me that story while I was out there I don't think I would have been able to cope. As it was I found it disturbing enough to think the media were pursuing my friends and relations in the hope of finding some dirt on me. I heard they'd even managed to root out my father in search of some juicy quotes. He later told me that some of them pursued him as he drove up the road on one of his motorbikes, but I think he gave them a pretty unquotable mouthful of abuse for their trouble.

Even though we were sitting in a luxurious, air-conditioned hotel, I still felt like a prisoner, because as long as they had my passport I couldn't get home to the children. I might not have been in prison but I still wasn't free. I phoned home often and Mahmoud would put the kids on the line. Each day I told them I would be back 'tomorrow', and each day I was proved to be a liar again when the authorities refused to give up their plans for prosecution and return our passports. I just couldn't bear the thought of telling them I didn't know when they would see their mummy again. But lying to them didn't feel any better. If everything went wrong and we ended up going to jail for three years I thought I could handle the physical hardships, but being without my children and thinking about them growing up without me would eat away at my insides and destroy me. I thought how Amira's hair would grow and I wouldn't be there to brush it for her; how Marlon would move on to big school and I wouldn't be there to prepare his new uniform with him and listen to his worries.

I found myself pining for the simplest things in my life. I missed just sitting on the sofa with a lovely, clean quilt cover and pillow, and sleeping. If I closed my eyes I could imagine Mahmoud waking me with a nice cup of tea. I imagined the smell of the kids when I kissed them goodnight and the sound of their voices coming down the street on their way home from school. When I dwelt on such thoughts I couldn't stop myself from crying.

One of my best friends from London, Mags, rang regularly. She was pregnant and had asked me to be the child's godmother once it arrived.

'It looks like I might not be back in time for the baby,' I said during one of the calls.

'Don't talk like that,' she said. 'If you're still there we'll all come out to you for the party. We'll bring out the champagne to wet the baby's head. But don't talk nonsense, of course you'll be back in time.' Her optimism cheered me up.

Among all the phone calls and messages I received I heard nothing from my mother. I sent her some flowers on her birthday to show I hadn't forgotten her but there was no response. People kept coming to the room with bouquets of flowers from well-wishers both in England and Dubai. It didn't seem as if everyone thought I was an evil woman.

Sarra had returned to her brittle, optimistic self once we got to the hotel, spending most of her days sunbathing by the swimming pool and the evenings with a strong Scotch. She seemed to assume that everything was now going to work out OK and that we'd soon all be on a plane home. She received a few calls from her family, who never exchanged any words with me if I happened to be the one who picked up the phone, but that was all. It sometimes felt as if I didn't exist in their lives at all. Her friend Jackie turned up to take her to a barbeque at her house. Apparently they'd been air hostesses together in their younger days and had stayed in touch. Jackie was mildly apologetic about not coming through with the passport when we needed it so desperately, but explained that her husband had forbidden it, not wanting to upset the Al-Habtoors. I think she said he was an Egyptian banker, or something along those lines, and couldn't afford to fall out with one of the richest families in the area. Sarra didn't seem to bear her any grudge and was obviously happy to be able to escape the hotel for a bit of socialising.

After watching Sarra in action in the various police stations and jails, and realising that her family barely acknowledged my existence, I knew that I couldn't rely on her or Neil to get me out of this situation. I was going to have to sort myself out with a lawyer, a defence and whatever else I needed. Otherwise Sarra was going to be going home, forgiven as the broken-hearted mother who'd just wanted to see her son, and I was going to be locked up for good as the 'professional kidnapper'.

After a few days we were moved to the Intercontinental Hotel. We always seemed to be being moved on to a new place by someone. I'd been trying to get through to Vicky on the phone in the jail, to find out how she was, and on the fourth day I succeeded. It felt so odd being on the outside when she was still in there. Her parents also came to visit us and I asked them to return the clothes I'd borrowed when they went to see her. Emotions and tensions were running high all around.

Neil was flown out to Dubai by the media to be with Sarra, and was filmed by the *Trevor McDonald* team being reunited with her at the hotel. They were interviewed by Colin Baker, the newsreader. The whole media circus was making me very nervous. I could just imagine how it would look to the public prosecutor with our story plastered all over the papers in England. It was going to sound as if we were criticising their system of justice, which was not likely to endear us to them. There was also a danger that they would read something about my past that would alert them to the fact that this might have been a planned job. I'd heard that the *Sunday Times* and other serious newspapers were running huge full-page stories about me, asking who I was and suggesting I was a professional kidnapper. That is not the sort of publicity you want when you are about to go to court for exactly that crime.

I was also uncomfortable with the fact that the television crew made Sarra and Neil re-enact their reunion hug three times in order to get it right for the cameras. It seemed so staged and false, not really news reporting, which was, I thought, the point of the story. Nothing seemed real or based on any genuine worry about Tariq's future, or discussion about whether it was better for him to be with his father or his mother. The focus had now shifted to Sarra and me and the question of whether we should be punished for what we'd done. It had all become one giant media event, way beyond anyone's control.

'Oh this is just amazing, we have to go on *Parkinson* with this. Look at these two,' Neil said to a man from *The Mail on Sunday*, pointing at Sarra and me. 'They're getting on so well. They're like soulmates.'

I kept quiet. I was now finding out from the British

journalists just what Neil had been saying to the papers before he came out. He'd been claiming that the kidnapping was planned but that he'd known nothing about it. He couldn't have said anything more incriminating for us, and less true about himself. He'd known what we were planning.

I was finding his behaviour more and more offensive. He kept making derogatory comments about Arabs. He knew that I was married to an Iraqi but it didn't seem to occur to him that every time he criticised Arabs he was criticising my husband and children.

Rashid's legal team were working hard to make sure that, whatever happened with the courts, Sarra was kept under control from then on. Papers were being drawn up for her to sign, promising never to attempt to take Tariq again. If she ever broke the contract she would lose all custodial rights over him. Sarra didn't want to sign anything and Nigel, who'd surrendered his passport and could now see his chances of getting it back receding, began to become nervous.

'Sign the papers, Sarra,' he said at one point. 'I want my passport back.'

'No, I'm sorry,' she replied. 'I'm not going to.'

'Donya's got a family she needs to get home to,' he pointed out. 'She has no hope of that until you sign.'

'Well, that's just the way it is,' Sarra said.

She did, however, agree to go to the British embassy and sign a gagging order saying she wouldn't talk to any press once she got back to England. Rashid was willing to give permission for her to go back home if she signed that. He also agreed to sign a paragraph saying that no charges would be pressed against me and, as far as he was concerned, I could go too. I thought that was very decent of him since I'd tried to take his son. Not many of the fathers I'd had dealings with would have been as understanding. Just because he'd agreed not to press charges personally, however, didn't mean the authorities would agree not to prosecute in order to make an example of us.

I was speaking to Mahmoud every evening and on one call he admitted that Khalid seemed to be getting sicker and had been taken into hospital. His words made my insides churn. I felt desperate at not being able to get back to my child when he needed me. How could I have spent so much time away and taken so many risks when one of my babies was ill? I felt wretched. And then I remembered that this was nothing compared to the agony that some of the mothers I'd helped had been through with their children. If I felt bad in my situation, I could barely imagine how they must have felt when they were forced to come looking for me in order to get their children back.

After a few days Neil went back to England and Sarra and I went in front of the chief public prosecutor once more. I was feeling very nervous after everything that had been going on in the media. I could see he was angry from the moment I walked through the door. Hazel, one of the women from the *Trevor McDonald* team, held my hand and squeezed it comfortingly as his laser-like eyes swivelled on to me. The feel of her fingers in mine reminded me of the counting game I played with Amira: one squeeze from me, two from her, three from me, four from her …

'You!' he shouted. 'No passport for you!'

I could feel every nerve and muscle in my body trembling. Hazel's hand squeezed mine and I could picture Amira standing beside me, looking up with those trusting, enquiring eyes. I felt sick. I kept imagining Khalid at home ill and in need of his mother, and my other children who hadn't seen me now for several weeks. Our lawyer looked as shocked as I felt and tried to reason with the prosecutor, but he wouldn't listen to any arguments. He'd made up his mind. I felt the tears coming and there was nothing I could do to stop them.

'We're checking you out through Interpol to see if you've done this sort of thing before,' he told me and from his expression it looked as if he expected to get enough information to put me away for years.

I was pretty sure that Interpol would have a fairly thick file on me by that time and it was beginning to sound as if Sarra would be able to get home and I wouldn't. As Hazel and I came out of the interview and told Sarra what had happened she seemed not to understand the gravity of my situation.

'You go back to your children,' I said. 'Don't worry about me.'

'All right,' she replied cheerily. 'I'll do that.'

I could see from the look on Hazel's face that she was shocked Sarra would even consider leaving me to my fate after I'd left my family and come out to help her. But Sarra didn't notice anything, she'd started chattering about some photographs of Tariq which she'd got at half price, holding them up to be admired. It seemed to me she'd completely lost touch with reality.

Back at the hotel I was receiving a stream of supportive phone calls and emails, even a letter from the hospital that was treating Khalid, confirming that he was ill and needed his mother. Sarra didn't get anything, apart from a couple of unpleasant messages from people who'd seen her on the *Trevor McDonald* show. There were articles appearing in the papers, which were nearly all supportive of what I was doing. Some of the mothers I'd helped in the past came forward and gave interviews. Kate Hamilton said some lovely things about me, calling me a 'living heroine' and saying I had a heart 'as big as the ocean', even though I still felt I'd let her down by only getting her an hour with her girls and failing to get them back for her. I was deeply moved by the tributes and the way in which my friends and people I'd never met were rallying behind me.

Mahmoud was quoted as calling me 'an angel without wings', which I think is the most romantic thing for him to say, particularly considering the hard time I give him and the amount of work I've caused him by going off and leaving him with the children so often.

While Sarra was happy to spend time visiting friends, relaxing by the pool or shopping with Neil, I spent every moment I could trying to contact people who could help me get home. I'd even phoned Rashid once or twice from the hotel, thanking him for being so reasonable and pleading with him to put in a word for us with the chief public prosecutor. I assured him how sorry I was.

'If it's any consolation,' I told him, 'Tariq didn't want to go with his mother, he wanted to stay with you.'

'Thank you for telling me that,' he said. 'I don't disapprove of what you do, you know. But I never kidnapped my son from his mother. They left Dubai of their own choice and they left him with me.'

I vowed to myself at that moment that I would never undertake another mission like this without doing far more investigation first. Although Rashid said he would drop all charges against me, he told me he didn't have any influence over the public prosecutor. He didn't seem to be too hopeful about our chances. We were going to have to look elsewhere if we wanted a white knight to ride to our rescue. We needed someone with even more power and influence than the Al-Habtoors, someone whose word was law.

'I want to write a letter to Sheik Al-Maktoum,' I said as we sat in the hotel room one morning trying to decide what to do next. 'You can type, Sarra, you help me.'

I knew that Al-Maktoum, as the all-powerful ruler of Dubai, would have the last word on whether I should be allowed to go home or not. I'd met him once, many years before, at a hotel in London when he'd been sitting at a table next to me in the coffee shop and was very nice to Marlon, who was small at the time. I remembered him seeming to be a kind man, someone who might respond to an appeal from the heart. Sarra claimed she had also been out with him, very briefly, before she met Rashid. The connections were tenuous, I couldn't deny that, but it seemed like a chance worth taking.

We went down to the computer room and I dictated a letter asking him for his help which Sarra typed up. It was more or less a begging letter. I apologised for disturbing the Al-Habtoor family and I promised never to do anything like it again if I was just allowed to return home to my family and my sick child. We printed up a copy, which Sarra put in her bag.

The following day Sarra and I were sitting in the hotel coffee shop with a lady from the law firm that I'd asked to help me. Living in a hotel, when you're waiting for something to happen, makes every hour of the day seem endlessly long and you are pathetically grateful for any distraction from the monotony. We were deep in conversation about what had been going on when there was a disturbance in the reception area outside the café. We looked up to see security men swarming everywhere and an entourage surrounding someone important sweeping towards one of the private dining rooms.

I realised it was Sheik Al-Maktoum and stood up to get a better view. He came close to where we were sitting and I caught his eye. He smiled and I smiled back. He then disappeared into the private room and his army of security men formed a human barrier at the entrance before I'd recovered myself enough to say anything.

'Where's the letter?' I asked Sarra.

'It's upstairs,' she said.

'Go and get it, quickly, now's our chance.'

A few minutes later she was back with the letter and we went to the doors that we'd just seen the Sheik disappearing through, but his army of security men barred our way.

'Please just give him this letter,' I pleaded.

'No.' They were adamant: stone faced, professional and

immovable. 'You have to go to the Sheikh's court if you wish to write to him and apply to have the letter given to him.'

'But that could take weeks!' I protested and they shrugged without smiling. There was, it seemed, no other way.

I begged and pleaded for a while, refusing to believe that I actually had to give up, but there was obviously nothing they could do. Realising we were getting nowhere we retreated back a few yards across the lobby and waited, like pop fans hanging around at a stage door for their idol to appear in the hope of catching his eye. Nothing happened for at least an hour, maybe two. Then a ripple of action amongst the security men alerted us to the fact that the doors were about to open. When they did and we saw the Sheik coming out into the lobby, I started jumping up and down and waving the letter in the air. I caught his attention and he changed direction, coming across towards us.

The bodyguards rushed over to move us out of his way but he told them to leave us alone.

'Yes, my dears?' he said.

'We have a letter for you,' the lawyer said.

'OK,' he said. 'Mr Kalifa will deal with this.' He indicated a man standing beside him. He then smiled sweetly and moved away to the exit where a fleet of cars was waiting for him. The man called Kalifa politely took the letter and dictated a mobile phone number, which I wrote quickly in my diary.

'Phone me in five minutes,' he said, before disappearing after the Sheik and the rest of the party.

We raced up to the bedroom and immediately called the

number. I could barely contain my excitement. What were the odds against a break like this happening? I couldn't believe our luck.

Kalifa answered the phone immediately. 'Sheik Al-Maktoum,' he told us matter-of-factly, 'says you can pick your passports up from the Attorney General tomorrow morning.'

It had worked. A shot in a million and we had hit the bullseye with it. I couldn't believe it. In fact I hardly dared believe it. All we had to go on was a voice on the phone. Supposing we got there the next day and no one knew anything about it? The more we protested that Sheik Al-Maktoum had said we could go, the more ridiculous it would sound. I spent an anxious night, trying to convince myself that I could sleep safely now.

The next morning, when I woke up from a fitful night, I suddenly felt that I couldn't get out of bed. It was as if my whole body had given up the fight. The strain and pressure had been so enormous for so many weeks that now it was lifted I realised I had no strength left. I was terrified of facing the chief public prosecutor again and of having him take away the chance we'd been given.

'I can't go,' I told the others. 'I can't move.'

I lay in bed, staring at the wall, waiting for something to happen. Eventually one of our lawyers rang to say he was at the police station and they were waiting for us to go and pick up the passports. I was going to have to make one last effort to keep going. I dragged myself out of bed and went down there with people on each side propping me up.

'Sign here, sign here,' the policeman said, as if it was the simplest business in the world, and then handed back our passports.

I was so relieved I thought I was going to weep.

'Where's my son's passport?' Sarra wanted to know, her voice ringing round the police station. 'He's a Fotheringham, not an Al-Habtoor. I want his passport with that name on it.'

I was so desperate to get out of that building and over to the airport, I could have throttled her. She was going to pick a fight with them now, when we were on the verge of escaping?

'Your son is an Al-Habtoor,' the official insisted politely but firmly. 'His passport stays with his father's family.'

Sarra continued protesting for a while, until the lawyers managed to quieten her down and get her out of the building.

On our way out the man from the human rights department came out of his office to see me, carrying boxes of chocolates for me to take home to my children, and some bags of Yemeni coffee for myself. He shook me by the hand and wished me well. I was touched by his thoughtfulness. My phone rang as we were driving back to the hotel. It was Mahmoud.

'Where's your passport now?' he asked.

'In my bag,' I told him.

'Don't open your bag for anyone,' he laughed. 'Come back as quickly as you can.'

I hardly remember the flight home. I was so exhausted I kept drifting in and out of consciousness, hardly taking in anything that was said to me. When I arrived back at Heathrow, Mahmoud was waiting for me with a giant bunch of flowers and news that Khalid was over the worst and coming home from hospital. I hugged him like I never wanted to let go.

Once I'd recovered my strength I got to look at some of the newspaper coverage there'd been while I was away. The British media had plastered my real name and picture all over their pages. My cover was blown. There was no point in keeping my identity a secret any more, but I was going to have to find a new way to help the women and children who'd been separated through no fault of their own. I might not be able to actually snatch back any more children myself, but I can still act as a trouble-shooter and go-between when families of different nationalities go to war over children. I will never be able to resist pleas for help from mothers who've lost their children.

The first day I went into school with the children I was very nervous about the reception I would receive. Although the staff of the school had sent messages of support to me in Dubai, there were many people there who would have had no idea about my past until they saw my face all over the papers, and I wasn't sure how they would react. I knew I had to brazen it out whatever happened, but I didn't want the children to witness any unpleasant scenes, or indeed be victimised themselves because of my beliefs. I needn't have worried. Everyone came up to say how hard they'd prayed for me while I was imprisoned, and to offer to help in any way they could in the future. I had truly arrived home.

Epilogue

IT WAS A PRODUCER on the *Trisha* show who first suggested I should write a book about my experiences. I'd been on the show and had been talking about some of my adventures in the green room afterwards. This was before I had met Sarra Fotheringham.

'I've been thinking about that,' I said, 'but I'm not sure I would be able to.'

'You need to find a ghostwriter to help you,' she said.

'I'll do that,' I said, suddenly decided, although I had no more idea how you set about finding a ghostwriter than flying to the moon.

I remembered reading a book called *Sold* by Zana Muhsen about how she and her sister had been sold by their father as child brides. She was a 15-year-old Birmingham girl at the time and had thought she was going to the Yemen for the holiday of a lifetime, only to find once she got there that the deal had been done and she wouldn't be going home to her family in Birmingham at the end of the holiday. She and her sister, Nadia, were then taken away into the mountains where they were treated as virtual slaves by their families-in-law. It took their mother about six years to find them and another two years to get Zana back to England. Nadia, I had heard, was still down there. The story, which had gripped me from page one and had made me weep several times, had been a huge bestseller around the world. I knew it was written in exactly the style I would want my own story told.

I went to the library and spotted it immediately in the biography section. The credit line said the ghostwriter was someone called Andrew Crofts. That, I decided, was the man I wanted to write my story but I had no idea how to find him. If, I decided, I could find missing children 2,000 miles away from home, this shouldn't be too difficult for me.

I found a list of publishing companies and rang the first one I recognised to ask them how I would set about tracking Andrew down. The editor who answered the phone asked me to tell him a bit about my story and, after hearing what I had to say, invited me in to talk to his colleagues. At the meeting they seemed very interested and suggested I try writing a synopsis of the book myself, so they could show it to their sales department and see if they could commission it. I went away and tried, encouraged by their enthusiasm, but it obviously wasn't working. If you're not a professional writer it's the hardest job in the world to order your thoughts, feelings and adventures into a coherent story. They read what I'd written and regretfully turned me down. I needed to renew my search for Andrew.

By this time I had become determined. I went back to the library and checked out the name of the firm that had published *Sold* and asked them how I could contact him. To my amazement they gave me his telephone number and within a few minutes I found myself telling him my story over the phone.

We agreed to meet and he came to see me at home. We were in one room, talking about the book, and Mahmoud was in another room, decorating, with the television on for company. When we heard him shouting at us to come downstairs I could tell there was an unusual urgency in his voice. Mahmoud is the calmest of men nearly all the time. We turned off the tape recorder and hurried down to see what was wrong. Mahmoud was standing in the middle of the room, his paintbrush still in his hand, the wall half-finished, staring at the television screen. The picture was of a plume of smoke emitting from one of the twin towers in New York. Horrified at the sight of what looked like a terrible accident we saw another plane appearing in the sky and a second explosion in the other tower. The gap between the two cultures that I live in had just become a canyon of unimaginable and horrible breadth. Although it would be some hours before anyone realised quite how enormous the repercussions of these actions were going to be, it was already obvious that this was a world-shattering event. As we watched the screen we heard that the Pentagon had also been attacked and it began to sound as if the whole world had gone mad. My thoughts immediately went to the children at school down the road, presumably still unaware of what was going on. How would this affect the rest of their lives?

The events which followed that terrible day seemed to make it even more important that I should write this book, to add my voice to the many others pleading for more understanding and consideration between the two cultures. One of the problems with writing the book, however, was going to be how to protect my own anonymity. I didn't want to open myself and my family up to the sorts of people who'd hissed those death threats down the line in Jordan, let alone the ones who'd organised the attack on America. The world did not seem a safe enough place to take such risks. But a few months later Sarra and I were plastered all over the papers and my name had become available to anyone who cared to look for it. The last reason for not writing the story had disappeared, and so Andrew and I set to work.

Now I have to decide what I want to do in the future. My ultimate dream at the moment, apart from continuing to bring up my family as well as I possibly can, is to open an orphanage in Iraq for some of the children I see hanging around the mosques in the hope of being given a few crusts of bread. I want to be able to provide them with somewhere safe to go and live out their childhoods, somewhere where they will be protected and loved and guided towards adult life. I also intend to raise money to finance mothers who want to go out to other countries to visit their children. It may be impractical for me to snatch children myself now, but that doesn't mean I can't still work to help bridge the gaps in these families, gaps that cause so much pain for all concerned.

By buying and reading this book you too have helped to move forward the cause of mutual understanding, and for that I thank you.